Cinderella Meets the Wolfman!

A Howlingly Funny Musical Spoof

Book by
Tim Kelly
Music & Lyrics by
Jack Sharkey

D1712732

A SAMUEL FRENCH ACTING EDITION

FOUNDED 1830
NEW YORK HOLLYWOOD LONDON TORONTO
SAMUELFRENCH.COM

ISBN 978-0-573-68158-5   Printed in U.S.A.   #5914

RENTAL MATERIALS

An orchestration consisting of **Piano Vocal Score** will be loaned two months prior to the production ONLY on the receipt of the Licensing Fee quoted for all performances, the rental fee and a refundable deposit.

Please contact Samuel French for perusal of the music materials as well as a performance license application.

IMPORTANT BILLING AND CREDIT
REQUIREMENTS

All producers of *CINDERELLA MEETS THE WOLFMAN!* *must* give credit to the Author of the Play in all programs distributed in connection with performances of the Play, and in all instances in which the title of the Play appears for the purposes of advertising, publicizing or otherwise exploiting the Play and/or a production. The name of the Author *must* appear on a separate line on which no other name appears, immediately following the title and *must* appear in size of type not less than fifty percent of the size of the title type.

STORY OF THE PLAY

Critics have hailed Tim Kelly and Jack Sharkey as "the masters of musical nonsense." This latest collaboration proves the point. They've taken the famous Cinderella story by the tail and given it a twist. The result is non-stop hilarity. In this version, the tiny kingdom of Vestigia is bankrupt, so the prince must marry money. The prince, by the way, is a werewolf. He's inherited the family curse from his ancestor Fuzzbrain the Seventh.

The court is adamant that the bride not discover the truth about her husband until after the wedding — or until her check clears. When Cinderella, "the fastest veggie-chopper in town" and her nasty sisters arrive on the scene, a full moon is on the rise. (Gypola, the matchmaker, plans to shoot the werewolf with a silver bullet and sell it to the Weird Museum — *stuffed!*)

From this point on the tune-filled laff riot takes off like a Roman candle. Paula Pond, Hollywood star, shows up to guide Cinderella on the royal road to romance, while Igor, the court jester, tries to remember who turned him into a chicken! (It's that kind of show.)

Not to worry. Everything turns out charming at the madcap finale. Wait 'til your audience sees the palace dance craze — "Doin' The Swine." Easy to produce with modern costumes, lots of small fun roles, and only one set. Delightful score, including such hits as "Have I Got A Girl For You," "My Night To Howl," "Magic Time," "If The Shoe Fits."

Suitable for all groups. This musical spoof is a real winner!

CHARACTERS
(In Order of Speaking)

(Castle staff, guests, villagers . . . chorus)

MUSICAL NUMBERS

OVERTURE

ACT ONE

BANKRUPTCY .... Chorus
SHE WON'T SUSPECT A THING . Snig, Snog, King, Queen
HAVE I GOT A GIRL FOR YOU! ...... Gypola, Vladimir,
Girls #1, #2, #3, Chorus
THE SMALLEST LITTLE COUNTRY
IN THE WORLD .... King, Queen
I'LL BE A PRINCESS ... Oleander, Ivy, Marriage Candidates
CHIN UP, HEAD HIGH! .... Cinderella, Chorus
THE MOMENT I SAW YOU .... Cinderella, Vladimir
MY NIGHT TO HOWL! .... Vladimir, Candidates

ENTR'ACTE

ACT TWO

IT WAS A WOLF ...... Palace Staff, Igor, Farmer, Peasants
HOLLYWOOD ROYALTY .... Paula, Male Admirers
MAGIC TIME .... Paula, Mitzi, Rodolpho, Cinderella
LOVELY PEOPLE, LOVELY WALTZ .... Ensemble
THE BEAST IN ME .... Mrs. Shrub, Ivy, Oleander
LOVELY PEOPLE, LOVELY—SWINE? ...... Cinderella,
Vladimir, Ensemble
IF THE SHOE FITS— .... Entire Company

6

SETTING

Castle Charming in the Kingdom of Vestigia, which is located west of Transylvania and east of the Frankenstein estates.

The time is the present.

ACT ONE

A late afternoon in summer.

ACT TWO

SCENE 1: Next day.
SCENE 2: The ball.

ABOUT THE PRODUCTION

For various suggestions on using a smaller cast; staging, costuming and accommodating the script to your individual requirements—consult NOTES at back of playbook.

Cinderella Meets the Wolfman

. ACT ONE

SETTING: The main assembly area of Castle Charming. It serves as throne room, ballroom and rec hall. US.C. *are two large throne-like chairs on a dais. There's a casement window positioned between the thrones, back somewhat. A bench is* S.L.; *another* S.R. *So much for the "basic" props. For suggestions on "dressing up" the stage picture consult PRODUCTION NOTES. Entrances and exits are* U.L., L., D.L., U.R., R., D.R. *AT RISE: VOICE of GUIDE from offstage,* R.

GUIDE. Follow me, please. There's a lot to see. Stay close.

(GUIDE enters R. *He wears a cap with "GUIDE" tacked on. With him are a gaggle of TOURISTS (can be all female). They have cameras and tour books. They gawk* L. *and* R.)

TOURISTS.
Golly,
Look at them big chairs.
First castle I've ever been in.
It looks like the lobby of the Paramount Thee-ater back home.
I'm gonna take me a picture.

(CASTLE STAFF enters U.R. *and* U.L. *as the GUIDE "lectures." CASTLE STAFF position themselves on either side of the thrones, stand at attention. TOURISTS flip the pages of their tour books, snap photos. GUIDE steps* C. *and TOURISTS move along with him.)*

GUIDE. You are now in the ancestral home of the Charmings, ruling family in the kingdom of Vestigia. (*TOURISTS, impressed, "Ooooh" and "Aaaaah".*) The royal family consists of King Charming, Queen Charming and their son and heir apparent, Prince Vladimir. Affectionately called by his loving and loyal subjects — "VLAD." (*TOURISTS applaud.*) To the west the castle is bordered by — (*points* L.) Transylvania.
TOURIST #1. That's vampire country! (*gasps*)

9

GUIDE. (*points* R.) To the east the castle is bordered by the estates of Baron Frankenstein.

TOURIST #2. That's monster country! (*more gasps*)

GUIDE. Castle Charming was founded in the tenth century. Everything is original.

TOURIST #3. Even the plumbing?

GUIDE. (*confirms*) Even the plumbing.

TOURIST #1. What's your chief export?

GUIDE. We have none.

TOURIST #2. What's your chief import?

GUIDE. We can't afford any.

TOURIST #3. What's the population?

GUIDE. Gets smaller every year.

TOURIST #1. What's the national debt?

GUIDE. Gets bigger every year.

TOURIST #2. What's the chief topic of conversation in Vestigia?

GUIDE. That's easy.

(*MUSIC INTROS, and GUIDE and CASTLE STAFF sing:*)

BANKRUPTCY
(Castle Staff, Guide)

(*NOTE: Vocal-level is indicated as the best way to indicate who sings what.*)

BARITONES. (*sing*)
BANKRUPTCY!
THE KINGDOM'S IN BANKRUPTCY!
EACH DEBTOR WHEN BILLS COME DUE
REFUSES OUR I.O.U.!

CONTRALTOS.
WE GOT NO CASH!
WE GOT NO DOUGH!
THE MARKET CRASH
HAS LEFT FINANCES LOW!

(*BARITONES/CONTRALTOS repeat in counterpoint; then:*)

TENORS.
OUR CREDITORS WILL BURY

US IN THE CEMETERY
IF OUR PRINCE DOESN'T MARRY
A LADY MILLIONAIRE!

(*BARITONES/CONTRALTOS/TENORS repeat in triple counterpoint; then:*)

SOPRANOS.
A ROYAL BALL'S THE ANSWER!
OUR PRINCE IS QUITE A DANCER,
AND SOME HONEY
WITH MONEY
HE MAY SWEEP OFF HER FEET!

(*ALL FOUR VOCAL GROUPS now do quadruple counterpoint-repeat; then:*)

ALL. (*including tourists*)
IF THEY BLEND
THERE'LL BE A SUDDEN END
TO BANKRUPTCY!
WHEE!

TOURIST #1. What's next on the tour? (*CASTLE STAFF briskly exits U.L. in a formal line.*)

GUIDE. Next, we will visit the royal kennels.

(*GUIDE and TOURISTS move to exit D.L. as IGOR thuds in from D.R. like an excited M.C. on a late night TV show.*)

IGOR. (*into audience, arms wide*) Here's Igor! (*TOURISTS turn, react, a TOURIST shrieks! Small wonder. IGOR is a weird sight. Half clown, half escapee from a horror film. He wears a jester's costume with some hides and pelts. His neck is a bit twisted and he has a hump. In one hand he carries a stick, attached to which are little bells.*)

TOURIST #1. Who's that?

TOURIST #2. What's that?

TOURIST #3. Let me get a picture. (*snaps*)

GUIDE. That's Igor. The court jester. He makes the king laugh.

TOURIST #1. The king must have a kinky sense of humor.

GUIDE. This way to the hounds. (*OTHERS start to exit, IGOR yells after them.*)

IGOR. I'm available for wedding anniversaries, kiddie parties and bar mitzvahs. Just telephone and leave a message on my machine.

(TOURISTS laugh, IGOR sticks out his tongue, shakes the bells. As TOURISTS exit, IGOR skips to the king's throne chair (s.r. side) sits. As he makes his u.s. cross, VOICES for off-stage r.)

QUEEN CHARMING. *(offstage)* It won't work, I tell you.
SNIG. *(offstage)* But, Your Majesty, we must be realistic.
QUEEN CHARMING. *(offstage)* What to do? What to do?
SNOG. *(offstage)* Carry out our plan, of course.
SNIG. *(offstage)* It's the only way.
KING. *(offstage)* I agree.

(Four enter. They are: KING CHARMING, QUEEN CHARM-ING, SNIG and SNOG. SNIG and SNOG are fussy, nervous types and whenever he's not being observed, IGOR imitates them. No one notices the jester. SNIG, SNOG, KING move c. Distraught, QUEEN paces, l., fools with her pearls. Every now and again she softly wails in way of comment on the conversation.)

SNIG. We have no other choice.
KING. Are you absolutely certain the kingdom is flat broke?
SNIG. As your First First Minister, I can state without fear of denial that the treasury is flatter than a turtle's tummy.
SNOG. As your Second First Minister, I can state without fear of denial that we haven't sold a postage stamp in years.
KING. Why not?
SNOG. We have no postal system.
KING. I forgot. Perhaps if we sold some wine?
SNOG. We have no grapes.
SNIG. We have nothing that anyone wants.
SNOG. If it weren't for the few tourists who manage to find their way here, Your Majesties would be out in the street. *(QUEEN CHARMING gasps, sits on bench.)*
KING. A terrible state of affairs. Terrible.
QUEEN. Lamentable. *(KING goes to his throne and, without noticing IGOR, sits.)*
KING. Auuugh. *(KING jumps up, sees IGOR.)* What are you doing on my throne?

IGOR. Playing a little joke.

KING. In that case why aren't I laughing?

IGOR. I don't know. Maybe you didn't sleep well. (*He gestures for IGOR to vacate the throne. IGOR scurries* R. *KING sits.*)

QUEEN. (*to IGOR*) His Majesty is in a grim mood. Be amusing, fool.

SNIG. You heard Her Majesty.

SNOG. Amuse!

IGOR. Amuse. Ah, yes. Amuse. (*Like a bad act on amateur night he "carries on."*) How's this— (*Razzle-dazzle*) Ah, what an occasion. This is what I've always dreamed of—playing the Palace. (*no reaction*) Heard it before, huh. (*thinking*) How about this one? (*enthusiastic*) When I was a baby I knew my mother didn't like me. She gave me a rattle—and the snake was still attached. (*again, no reaction. Frantic:*) Would you like to see a tap dance? (*He takes out a water faucet tap on the end of a string and "dances" it about. OTHERS stare, deadpan.*) Anyone interested in card tricks?

QUEEN. He's not the least bit funny. (*In way of protest IGOR shakes his head, curtsies to QUEEN. He turns his back and makes an angry face.*) We ought to get rid of him. (*IGOR is livid.*)

SNIG. Always the same old jokes.

SNOG. He couldn't make a hyena laugh.

IGOR. (*to audience*) Speaking of old jokes.

SNOG. Have you no pride? (*IGOR nods that he does, takes out a bottle of soap detergent, or furniture polish, the label reading "Pride," and gleefully displays it to audience and to SNOG. OTHERS groan.*)

SNIG. It costs to feed the fool, Your Majesty. A waste of money.

SNOG. A waste of food.

IGOR. (*to audience, deflated*) It's a tough house. (*He sulks off,* R.)

KING. A rich bride for the prince is the only way to save Vestigia!

SNIG. Check.

SNOG. Double check.

QUEEN. (*stands*) Don't mention "checks." We have them bouncing all over Europe. Oh, the shame! Oh, the scandal! Oh, the disgrace!

SNOG. Think positive.

QUEEN. How can I with disaster staring us in the face?

KING. Look the other way.

SNIG. A rich bride and all your problems are over.

QUEEN. (*suddenly forceful*) Men! You all think alike. Money solves everything.

KING. It certainly helps.

QUEEN. Marry off the prince and that's that.

MALES. That's that.

QUEEN. The problem is solved.

MALES. Solved. (*QUEEN folds her arms and taps one foot.*)

QUEEN. And what about the "other" problem? What do you propose to do about that?

MALES. Other problem?

QUEEN. Have you forgotten? (*pause*) Vlad has the Charming "Curse." (*OTHERS cringe.*) Vlad is handsome and Vlad is good but when the moon is full he turns into a— (*swallows*) I can hardly bring myself to say it.

KING. Then don't.

QUEEN. (*blurts it out*) A wolf!

KING. You said it.

SNIG. The furry kind.

SNOG. With fangs.

KING. (*shrugs*) We must be philosophical about these things. So, the prince is a werewolf. No one's perfect. (*QUEEN moves up beside the KING. SNIG and SNOG cross to the benches, one L., one R.*)

QUEEN. What do you think a girl will do when she discovers her future husband is as likely to *bite* her as kiss her? That he prefers gnawing on a bone to watching television.

KING. (*crosses his leg, ponders the situation*) I hadn't thought of that. Hmmmmmmmm.

QUEEN. You better think about it. (*to SNIG*) And you. (*to SNOG*) And you.

KING. The Queen is right. We're all in this together. Sink or swim. We either save Vestigia or line up for food stamps.

QUEEN. What a calamity!

SNIG & SNOG. Hmmmmmmmmm. (*SNIG and SNOG, a finger to the temple, crisscross as they also "ponder".*)

KING. Hmmmmmmmmm.

SNIG. Hmmmmmmmmm.

SNOG. Hmmmmmmmmm.

SNIG. *I have it!* (*OTHERS stiffen.*)

QUEEN. Well? (*SNIG reconsiders whatever it was he was going to suggest.*)

SNIG. On second thought, it wouldn't work. (*Again, SNIG and SNOG crisscross as they continue "to think".*)

SNOG. How about — ?

OTHERS. Yes?

SNOG. (*reconsiders, shakes his head*) It wouldn't work, either.

KING. (*about to suggest something*) Perhaps, if — ?

OTHERS. Yes, yes.

KING. (*rejects whatever it was he had to propose*) Forget it. (*SNIG and SNOG crisscross once more, lost in thought.*)

SNIG. *Aha!*

OTHERS. Well?

SNIG. True, the problem is staring us in the face, but so is the solution.

QUEEN. We're listening.

SNIG. Look at it this way, Your Majesties. Once the prince marries, your financial worries are over. The kingdom is saved and everyone is hap, hap, happy. But if we tell the prospective bride the truth, she won't go through with the wedding.

KING. She must!

SNIG. Then say nothing. Why step on a good thing?

SNOG. Bravo! With any luck, she won't find out until it's too late.

KING. Good thinking.

QUEEN. Then the wedding is on!

(*MUSIC INTROS. KING and QUEEN step c. to join SNIG and SNOG. All sing:*)

SHE WON'T SUSPECT A THING

SNIG. (*sings*)
SHE WON'T SUSPECT A THING!
KING/QUEEN.
NOT A THING!
SNOG.
SO WHEN THE CHURCH BELLS RING . . .

SNIG/QUEEN.
DINGALING!
KING.
NO REASON SHE SHOULD LOSE HER NERVE!

QUEEN.
SHE WON'T KNOW SHE'S A HOT *HORS D'OEUVRE!*
SNIG.
THERE DARE NOT BE A DOUBT . . .
KING/QUEEN.
. . . IN HER HEAD!
SNOG.
LET'S HOPE SHE WON'T FIND OUT . . .
SNIG/QUEEN.
. . . ERE THEY WED . . .
KING.
. . . THAT WHEN SHE DONS THE BRIDAL TRAIN . . .
QUEEN.
. . . SHE'S LIVING IN THE FAST-FOOD LANE!
ALL.
IF SHE'S NOT A COWARD, SHE WON'T HAVE A CARE:
WHEN SOMEONE'S DEVOURED YOUR FEET,
YOU'RE WALKING ON AIR!
SNIG.
THEY'LL DRAIN THE BRIDAL CUP . . .
KING/QUEEN.
. . . AT THE FEAST!
SNOG.
BUT WHEN THE MOON COMES UP . . .
SNIG/QUEEN.
. . . IN THE EAST . . .
KING.
. . . THE BRIDE WILL LEARN IN NOTHING FLAT . . .
QUEEN.
. . . A WAY TO LOSE UNWANTED FAT!
ALL.
SINCE VLAD'S WEIRD NUTRITION
LEAVES NOT MUCH TO CLEAR,
WE'LL TELL THE MORTICIAN
WE'LL JUST NEED A SHORT BIER!
SNIG.
HER PASSING WE SHALL GRIEVE . . .
KING/QUEEN.
. . . THROUGH THE TOWN!
SNOG.
THE CASH THAT SHE WILL LEAVE . . .

SNIG/QUEEN.
. . . TO THE CROWN . . .
KING.
. . . WILL BUY SOME STOCK . . .
QUEEN.
. . . AND OUT OF HOCK . . .
KING/QUEEN.
. . . WE'LL SOON BE EXITING!
SNIG/QUEEN.
OUR TREASURY'S A BUST!
KING/QUEEN.
LACKADAY!
SNIG/SNOG.
SO TAKE A BRIDE HE MUST!
KING/QUEEN.
RIGHT AWAY!
ALL.
HE'LL HAVE HIS PRINCESS *A LA KING!*
SHE WON'T SUSPECT A THING!

(*VLAD enters* L., *a rather handsome young man. We like him at once. On one hand he wears a large ring.*)

SNIG & SNOG. Prince Vladimir. (*SNIG and SNOG bow.*)
VLAD. Hello, Snig. Hello, Snog. Hello, Father. Hello, Mother.
QUEEN. My boy. You look pale.
VLAD. I've got a lot on my mind.
KING. You've thought it over.
VLAD. (*resigned*) If marrying a rich girl is what you want, I am willing to sacrifice myself. (*Pleased, OTHERS applaud.*) Still, I had hoped to marry for love.
SNIG. Who's talking about love?
SNOG. We're talking about marriage.
VLAD. Oh, Snig. Oh, Snog. That's cynical.
KING. (*insists*) We're talking about saving Vestigia!
QUEEN. Vladimir, think only of our kingdom. One day you will rule. Vestigia must be preserved.
VLAD. It won't be easy to find a girl who'll accept a wolfman — even if he has a title.
OTHERS. Sssssssh.
QUEEN. You will say nothing about the curse.

VLAD. Is that fair to my bride?

SNIG. That's her problem.

SNOG. Think of the curse as an adolescent inconvenience — like acne.

VLAD. Acne!?

(*Voice of GYPOLA rings out from offstage* R.)

GYPOLA. (*offstage*) Nothing to worry about, darlinks! Gypola always gets her girl!

QUEEN. (*looks* R.) Now what?

KING. (*looks* R.) It's the matchmaker. That gypsy hag, Gypola. I don't trust her. She can lie without moving her lips.

(*GYPOLA enters.*)

GYPOLA. At your service, darlinks. (*She bows. GYPOLA is the classic operatic cliche of a gypsy hag. Outrageous. Her costume is a rainbow of clashing colors. A scarf on her head, a fringed shawl over her shoulders, flashing earrings and enough bangles, baubles and beads to stock a boutique.*)

SNIG. You've lined up some candidates?

GYPOLA. I've been scattering Polaroids of the prince like candy samples. Up one street and down the other.

VLAD. (*embarrassed*) It's so demeaning. (*Depressed, he crosses to bench,* L., *sits.*)

SNOG. Remember, Gypola, she must be rich.

SNIG. Very rich.

KING. Extravagantly rich.

QUEEN. If she has a gold card from American Express, we'll settle for that.

VLAD. (*wavering*) I don't know if I can go through with this.

KING. What?

QUEEN. You must.

SNIG. Think of the kingdom.

SNOG. Think of Vestigia.

GYPOLA. Think of my commission.

QUEEN. Vladimir, you must pull yourself together.

KING. Duty commands.

GYPOLA. (*to KING and QUEEN*) Let me handle this. I know my business.

QUEEN. Don't fail us.

GYPOLA. Never fear. Gypola's here. (*KING gives his arm to QUEEN and they stately exit* U.L. *followed by SNIG and SNOG.*)

VLAD. If only I weren't a romantic. If only I could be hard and realistic.

GYPOLA. Don't look so glum, my princeling. (*She takes him by the hand and leads him to the KING's throne.*) When you see what I've brought to the castle, you'll smile and thank me a million times over. (*VLAD sits.*) Comfy? (*He nods, GYPOLA calls* R.) We're waiting, darlinks. Best foot forward. Front and center!

(*She produces a whistle, blows a shrill blast. Immediately, three marriage CANDIDATES, giggling, run in and move in front of bench,* R. *In unison, they curtsy.*)

MARRIAGE CANDIDATES. Your Majesty.
VLAD. Ladies.
GYPOLA. (*to VLAD*) So pick.
VLAD. A wife is not a vegetable, Gypola.
GYPOLA. Unless she's a tomato.

(*MUSIC INTROS. GYPOLA sings:*)

HAVE I GOT A GIRL FOR YOU!

GYPOLA. (*in plaintive, minor-keyed Gypsy-style:*)
IT IS NOT EASY TO DECIDE,
WHEN ONE MUST FIND A PROPER BRIDE!
SO LET ME HELP YOU, IF I MAY,
IN MY SEDATE OLD GYPSY WAY . . . !
(*Blows another shrill blast. Simultaneously with a* loud *musical pep-rally fanfare, CHORUS members enter with pompons and then as they wave pompons cheerily, GYPOLA launches into sales talk-song:*)
HAVE I GOT A GIRL FOR YOU!
(*#1 moves up.*)
  CHORUS.
OH, GOLLY!
  GYPOLA.
HAIR OF GOLD AND EYES OF BLUE!
  CHORUS.
HOW JOLLY!

GYPOLA.
HOW COULD YOUR HEART RESIST FINDING HER
 DEAR,
AND PRESSING HER NEAR,
WHILE NIBBLING ON HER EAR?!
CHORUS.
HAS SHE GOT A GIRL FOR YOU!
GYPOLA.
A CUTIE!
CHORUS.
JUST RIGHT FOR A RENDEZVOUS!
GYPOLA.
HER BEAUTY
CERTAINLY PROMISES HEAVEN FOR TWO!
HAVE I GOT A GIRL FOR YOU!
CHORUS.
YOU! YOU! YOU!

(*MUSIC switches to "interview-theme" (as it will each time
 VLAD begins to sing), as VLAD gives once-over to #1,
 during:*)

VLAD.
LET THE LITTLE LADY GIVE ME MORE DETAILS.
GIRL #1.
I AM SWEET, SERENE AND FREE OF CARES!
VLAD.
TELL ME, THEN, WHY DO YOU BITE YOUR
 FINGERNAILS?
GIRL #1.
'CAUSE NO ONE ELSE WILL LET ME CHEW ON THEIRS!
VLAD. (*reacts*)
I'M FEELING QUEASY!

*And (as after every interview-theme segment) we go right back to
 an increasingly frantic GYPOLA, who quickly brings next
 girl forward as the first returns to bench, sits, etc.*)

GYPOLA.
NEVER MIND, HERE'S NUMBER TWO!
CHORUS.
BEHOLD HER!

GYPOLA.
SHE'S THE PERFECT GIRL FOR YOU!
CHORUS.
ENFOLD HER!
GYPOLA.
OH, WHAT A DARLING DELIGHT TO THE EYE,
EXCITING BUT SHY,
WITH LIPS LIKE CHERRY PIE!
CHORUS.
WHAT A GORGEOUS GIRL FOR YOU!
GYPOLA.
SO STUNNING!
CHORUS.
CAST YOUR VOTE FOR NUMBER TWO!
GYPOLA.
HER CUNNING
WAYS AND HER WINSOMENESS BRIGHTEN THE VIEW!
SHE'S SURELY THE GIRL FOR YOU!
CHORUS.
YOU! YOU! YOU!
VLAD.
DON'T YOU HAVE A TINY TENDENCY TO FAT?
(*He's being polite; she is a junior blimp*)

GIRL #2.
BUT I WORK OUT DAILY ON MY BIKE!
VLAD.
STILL, YOU'RE RATHER HIPPY. WHAT'S THE CAUSE
   OF THAT?
GIRL #2.
I NEVER MET A MEAL I DIDN'T LIKE!
VLAD.
I CAN'T AFFORD HER!
(*starts to exit*)

GYPOLA. (*stops him*)
PLEASE DON'T GO, HERE'S NUMBER THREE!
CHORUS.
VIVACIOUS!
GYPOLA.
FINE OF FORM AND FANCY-FREE!
CHORUS.
FLIRTATIOUS!

GYPOLA. (*her mind going slightly, can't control her imagery*)
SOFTER THAN SAUERKRAUT, SILKEN OF SKIN!
ATTRACTIVELY THIN,
WITH JUST A SINGLE CHIN!
    CHORUS.
SHE'S YOUR FINAL INTERVIEW!
    GYPOLA.
I PROMISE!
    CHORUS.
THIS ONE'S RIFE WITH REVENUE!
    GYPOLA.
HER MOMMA'S
LOADED WITH LUCRE AND ELDERLY, TOO!
CAN SHE BE THE GIRL FOR YOU?
    CHORUS.
YOU! YOU! YOU!
    VLAD.
I'LL ADMIT SHE'S LOVELY! MAYBE THIS IS IT!
    GIRL #3.
FOR YOUR CULTURE I'M DESIGNED TO PLEASE!
    VLAD.
COULD YOU CLARIFY THAT JUST A LITTLE BIT?
    GIRL #3.
I YODEL ROCK-AND-ROLL IN JAPANESE!
    VLAD. (*palm to forehead, lurches toward wings*)
I'VE GOT A HEADACHE!
    GYPOLA. (*desperately blocks his path*)
DON'T GIVE UP SO EASILY!
    VLAD.
I'M STRICKEN!
    GYPOLA.
WON'T YOU PICK A BRIDE-TO-BE?
    VLAD.
I'M CHICKEN!
    GYPOLA/CHORUS.
YOU ONLY NEED A PUSH!
DON'T BEAT AROUND THE BUSH!
    GYPOLA.
HAVE I GOT A GIRL . . .
    CHORUS.
TO BE YOUR BRIDE!

GYPOLA.

. . . FOR . . .

CHORUS.

YOU MUST DECIDE!

GYPOLA.

. . . YOU!

CHORUS.

HAS GYPOLA GOT A GIRL FOR YOU!

(*CHORUS exits. The three CANDIDATES are standing, grinning at VLAD, hopeful. GYPOLA steps close to VLAD.*)

GYPOLA. They like you. (*stage whisper*) They're rich, remember. *Rich.*

VLAD. (*evasive*) I can't decide now. (*As GYPOLA continues to speak to VLAD she indicates CANDIDATES should withdraw. Disappointed, they frown, curtsy, exit R.*)

GYPOLA. I understand. You want to make your choice known tomorrow night. At the ball. A good idea. (*to audience*) Helps to build suspense.

(*KING and QUEEN return.*)

KING. Any luck?

VLAD. Depends on what you mean by luck.

GYPOLA. These things takes time.

QUEEN. Vestigia has no time.

GYPOLA. Come along, my princeling. Meet the others.

VLAD. You mean there are more?

GYPOLA. More is better.

KING. You WON'T fail, Gypola?

GYPOLA. (*offended at the suggestion*) Would this face lie? (*GYPOLA leads VLAD R. He looks longingly to his mother.*)

VLAD. Maybe if we built a hotel tourists would stay overnight in Vestigia.

QUEEN. Build a hotel?

KING. There isn't room.

VLAD. How about a MacDonald's? (*GYPOLA gives a hard yank and VLAD practically flies offstage.*)

(*MUSIC INTROS and KING and QUEEN sing to audience:*)

THE SMALLEST LITTLE COUNTRY IN THE WORLD
(King, Queen)

KING.
WE'RE PROUD OF OUR LAND, WHAT THERE IS OF IT.
QUEEN.
IT'S NOT VERY GRAND, BUT STILL WE LOVE IT.
BOTH.
"THE SMALLEST LITTLE COUNTRY IN THE WORLD," I
  SWEAR IT'S TRUE!
OR, AS WE ABBREVIATE IT: "THE S. L. C. IN THE W."!
(*This is sung as "ess-ell-cee in the dub-ull-yoo" of course.*)
KING.
WHERE ELSE DOES THE NATIONAL ARENA
HOLD A TOTAL OF FORTY-TWO,
OR A HUNDRED FEET WALK THE ONE-WAY STREET?
TRY THE S. L. C. IN THE W.!
QUEEN.
WHERE ELSE CAN THEY SERVE YOU A SUBPOENA
WITHOUT CROSSING THE AVENUE,
AND THE PHONE BOOK GIVES ONLY RELATIVES?
IT'S THE S. L. C. IN THE W.!
KING.
WHEN YOU DALLY AT MAH-JONGG,
YOU GET A SINGLE TILE TO PLAY!
QUEEN.
IF A TOURIST COMES ALONG,
SOMEBODY ELSE MUST GO AWAY!
KING.
THE ZOO HAS ONE DESOLATE HYENA;
HE'S SO LONELY, HE SIGHS "BOO-HOO!"
AND HIS CAGE WOULD CRAMP ANY POSTAGE STAMP,
IN THE S. L. C. IN THE W.!
LEAVE YOUR DINNER ON THE STOVE;
IT CANNOT BURN IF YOU SHOULD ROAM . . .
QUEEN.
. . . FOR, WHEREVER YOU MAY ROVE,
YOU'RE ONLY HALF A MILE FROM HOME!
BOTH.
OUR LOVE FOR OUR FLAG WOULD BE MUCH KEENER
IF IT EVER COULD BE UNFURLED!
IF WE EVER VIEWED IT,
WE'D MAKE ROOM TO SALUTE IT,
AND HALF A BATON WOULD BE TWIRLED!
WE SWEAR WE WOULDN'T KID YA:

SARDINES AVOID VESTIGIA,
THE   SMALLEST   LITTLE   COUNTRY   IN   THE
WORLD . . . !

(*The gentleness of the moment is shattered by the whoops, hollers,
shrieks   of   MARRIAGE   CANDIDATES   and   their
MOTHERS.*)

QUEEN. (*looks* R.) *What on earth —? (VLAD, fleeing in terror,
dashes onstage.*)
VLAD. They're heading this way! The marriage candidates and
their mothers.
QUEEN. Mothers!
KING. They sound dangerous. We'd better withdraw. (*KING
and QUEEN hurry out,* D.L. *VLAD escapes* U.L.)

(*In thunder, from* R., *the MARRIAGE CANDIDATES and their
"stage" MOTHERS. Included in the excited mob, are the
haughty MRS. SHRUB and her two husband-hunting daughters, IVY and OLEANDER. They are rather stupid and have
squeaky voices and giggle a lot. NOTE: For an antic bit of
casting these two roles, in the British tradition of Christmas
pantomime, might be portrayed by male actors.*)

IVY. Aw! He's getting away!
OLEANDER. Anyone would think the prince was afraid of us.
MRS. SHRUB. Don't be absurd, daughters dear. Prince Vladi-
mir was overwhelmed by your beauty and ran off to compose
himself.
OTHERS. Ha!
IVY. I want to be married!
OLEANDER. Me, too!
IVY. I want a husband!
OLEANDER. Any husband will do! (*MRS. SHRUB is furious
with them. She grabs OLEANDER and gives her a good shaking.*)
MRS. SHRUB. Any husband will do?! Have you lost your
senses? Don't be foolish, don't be stupid. (*OLEANDER stares
blankly into audience as her mother continues to shake her as if
she were a large rag doll.*)
IVY. Better let her go, Mama. She's all shook up. (*MRS.
SHRUB releases OLEANDER, who continues to shake on her
own for a few more seconds.*)

MRS. SHRUB. Just *any* husband will not do. Pay attention, Ivy. Listen to every syllable, Oleander.

OLEANDER. What's a syllable?

MRS. SHRUB. *Pay attention, I said!*

IVY & OLEANDER. (*curtsy*) Yes, Mama. (*MRS. SHRUB draws her daughters close. OTHERS "eavesdrop."*)

MRS. SHRUB. Ever since your stepfather— (*out to the audience, emphasizing the plot point*) —my *second* husband— (*back to daughters*) —went up in a balloon and never came down, I've had to be mother and father to you both.

IVY & OLEANDER. Yes, Mama.

MRS. SHRUB. Have I ever complained?

IVY & OLEANDER. No, Mama.

MRS. SHRUB. Have I ever made demands?

IVY & OLEANDER. No, Mama.

MRS. SHRUB. I've even had to care and feed my second husband's wretched daughter. What's her name? I never can remember it.

IVY & OLEANDER. (*high-pitched voices*) Cinderella.

MRS. SHRUB. That's it. Cinderella. Ugh. Sounds like a soda pop. (*smiles like a cobra*) It's time for one of you girls to do something for me.

IVY & OLEANDER. Yes, Mama?

MRS. SHRUB. Make me proud. Make me the mother of—a princess. (*IVY & OLEANDER giggle in girlish fashion.*) That shouldn't be too hard. (*lifts her voice so OTHERS are sure to hear*) After all, I am the *richest* widow in the kingdom of Vestigia and money talks.

GIRL #1. (*on the defensive*) He'll pick me!

GIRL #2. Me!

GIRL #3. I'll be the lucky one.

MRS. SHRUB. Time will tell.

(*IVY and OLEANDER giggle again. MRS. SHRUB steps to MOTHERS and they "talk." MARRIAGE CANDIDATES group together as MUSIC INTROS, sing:*)

I'LL BE A PRINCESS
(Marriage Candidates)

ALL.
I'LL BE A PRINCESS SEATED ON A DAINTY LITTLE

THRONE
GAZING ABOUT IN ROYAL SPLENDOR!
IN A HOME OF SHINING TOWERS,
SIPPING FROM A SILVER SPOON!
    IVY.
I WILL PARTY TILL ALL HOURS,
AND REMAIN IN BED TILL NOON!
    ALL.
QUITE SOON . . .
    OLEANDER.
. . . I'LL BE A PRINCESS, WITH A WEE WINE CELLAR
    OF MY OWN,
WHERE I'LL GO ON A ROYAL BENDER!
(*Teetotallers: For latter two lines, substitute:*)
(. . . I'LL BE A PRINCESS, WITH A MASERATI OF MY
    OWN,
EM'RALDS AND PEARLS UPON EACH FENDER!)
    ALL.
I'LL INDULGE IN HAPPY HUGGING ON THE PRINCE'S
    ROYAL KNEE!
GEE . . .
I'LL BE A PRINCESS, WAIT AND SEE!
    IVY.
I'LL DINE ON BLINTZES UNDERNEATH A PRETTY
    PARASOL!
    OLEANDER.
I'LL HAVE A HORSE AND GOLDEN CARRIAGE!
    IVY. (*to OLEANDER, huffily*)
EVEN SUNK IN DEEP DESPAIR, HE'D
NEVER CHOOSE YOU OVER ME!
    OTHERS. (*to both of them*)
WANNA BET HE'LL HAVE YOU BURIED
UNDERNEATH HIS FAM'LY TREE?!
    ALL.
TRULY . . .
I'LL BE A PRINCESS, ONCE HE MEETS ME AT THE PAL-
    ACE BALL!
HE'LL OFFER ME A ROYAL MARRIAGE!
AND WHEN HE HAS INTRODUCED ME TO HIS ROYAL
MA AND PA . . .
AH . . .
I'LL BE A PRINCESS, TRA-LA-LA!

Ivy.
ANTICIPATION HAS ME QUAKING!
OLEANDER.
I'M BRACING FOR THE UNDERTAKING!
ALL.
I HOPE HIS HIGHNESS WILL BE MAKING
ME A ROYAL PRINCESS TODAY,
AND PRINCESS I'LL STAY!

(*SNIG enters* L.)

SNIG. Welcome to Castle Charming, ladies.
IVY. He's cute.
OLEANDER. You married?
MRS. SHRUB. Oleander!
SNIG. Your rooms have been prepared. You'll be crammed but you'll manage. (*A great squeal of delight from the females as they practically knock down poor old SNIG as they exit.*)
MRS. SHRUB. (*yells* R.) *Hurry up, Cinderella! You lazy girl! Bring the luggage!*

(*MRS. SHRUB follows after the OTHERS and we hear the off-stage voice of CINDERELLA.*)

CINDERELLA. (*offstage*) I'm hurrying as fast as I can, Stepmother.

(*Pause for effect and, then— Enter Cinderella. At first we can't tell much about her because her back is bent and her face down — due to the small mountain of luggage she is carrying. Her dress is mostly rags (if the actress can manage it, she might be barefooted). SNIG, fascinated, watches her crablike progression across the stage. She punctuates her cross with little gasps for breaths, softly exclaiming from the burden: "Oh"— "Ah"— "Ooow." She bumps into SNIG.*)

SNIG. Watch where you're going. (*Startled, CINDERELLA drops the luggage.*)
CINDERELLA. Oh, I am sorry, sir. It's all my fault. (*curtsy*) Please forgive me.

(*We get a good look at her and discover she's enchanting; petite, wide-eyed, lovely. Beneath that smudged face— beauty!*)

SNIG. (*incredulous*) You're not one of the marriage candidates?

CINDERELLA. Of course not, sir. I could never aspire to such a hope. I'm a kitchen slavey. I also feed the chickens and slop the hogs.

SNIG. That's an odd-looking dress you're wearing.

CINDERELLA. It's last year's. (*to audience*) And the year before that.

SNIG. (*studying the "dress," bewildered*) What's that material?

CINDERELLA. Dishcloth.

SNIG. What's the color?

CINDERELLA. Soot.

SNIG. Soot?

CINDERELLA. I sleep in my stepmother's fireplace. In the kitchen. With the cat. I never complain. (*to audience*) At least it's warm and I'm close to the pots and pans. (*to SNIG*) You see, my first name is Ella.

SNIG. Ella, yes.

CINDERELLA. No. Ella Shrub. But I'm always covered with cinders. (*Eyelashes blinking, she stares into the audience.*) That's why they call me Cinderella.

(*Attracted by the sight of this odd girl, CHORUS members appear, listen and watch. NOTE: Director can use CASTLE STAFF; TOUR GUIDE, SNOG, even IGOR.*)

SNIG. (*disapprovingly*) Your father allows you to sleep in a fireplace?

CINDERELLA. (*eyes cast down*) He's gone, sir. Never to be seen again. He was an adventurer. Up in a balloon and blown away.

SNIG. Ah, yes. I seem to recall that gentleman. Eccentric.

CINDERELLA. No, sir. His name was Walter. Must get the rest of the luggage. (*As she talks, and the OTHERS stare, CINDER-ELLA runs off* D.R., *only to return immediately dragging a wicker hamper or wooden chest. NOTE: The hamper or chest must be strong enough to sit on. If CINDERELLA needs assistance a CHORUS member will help.*) My sisters are both so anxious to marry they want to look their best. I've had to pack everything they had in the closet. Jewels, hose, shoes, fans, corsets, gowns. Besides being a kitchen slavey, I'm a seamstress. I can sew, mend and patch. And when it comes to chopping veggies I'm the best in Vestigia. (*The hamper/chest is positioned* D.C. *Exhausted, CIN-DERELLA sits.*) A moment to catch my breath.

SNIG. You cook, you sew, you keep house. (*to CHORUS*)

What an exceptional girl. (*to CINDERELLA*) What's your pay?
CINDERELLA. (*into audience, smiling*) What's pay?
SNOG. Despite all, she seems a cheerful creature.
SNIG. Either that or she's an airhead.

(*MUSIC INTROS. CINDERELLA, suddenly brimful of energy, jumps up, and sings*:)

CHIN UP, HEAD HIGH!
(Cinderella, Chorus)

CINDERELLA.
CHIN UP! HEAD HIGH!
SUN'LL ERUPT IN THAT LEADENING SKY!
WHEN THINGS GO AMISS,
SIMPLY PRETEND YOU'RE BLISSFUL!
CHEST OUT! STAND TALL!
WHAT IF THE RAIN SHOULD CONTINUE TO FALL?
RAINDROPS BRING THE FLOWERS,
SO BLESS THE SHOWERS THAT SQUALL!
CHORUS.
ALTHOUGH
THERE'S MUD IN THE LANE CLUTTERED WITH
  GARBAGE
SO
THE CRUDDY TERRAIN WON'T LET THE CAR BUDGE,
NO
FESTERING CESSPOOL SHOULD
PREVENT YOUR FEELING GOOD!
CINDERELLA.
THOUGH SLIME'S CONGEALING—
CINDERELLA/CHORUS.
—EACH DROP
HELPS THE PEACH CROP!
CINDERELLA.
BRAVE SMILE! STOUT HEART!
SOMEDAY THE THUNDER AND FOG WILL DEPART!
CHORUS.
THOUGH WOES PILE UP—
CINDERELLA.
—DON'T GET YOUR BILE UP—
CINDERELLA/CHORUS.
—JUST KEEP THAT SMILE UP

ALL DAY!

(*Now, all dance, with CINDERELLA cheerily going from one man to another, etc., and as dance nears end, they continue:*)
DON'T BE
MOPY!
SMILES CAN DROWN
THOSE MAGGOTS OF AGONY DRAGGIN' YOU DOWN!

(*DANCE ENDS, but SONG CONTINUES:*)
    CINDERELLA.
SQUARE THOSE SHOULDERS!
    CHORUS.
TWIDDLE YOUR NOSE AT EACH COLD THAT OCCURS!
    CINDERELLA.
STAND FAST!
    CHORUS.
DON'T RECLINE!
    ALL.
SOMEWHERE THE SUN IS SHINING!
    CINDERELLA.
CHEER UP! THINK BIG!
    CHORUS.
THERE IS NO FUTURE IN FLIPPIN' YOUR WIG!
    CINDERELLA.
GLOOM'S SO INFANTILE!
    CHORUS.
IN A LITTLE WHILE—
    CINDERELLA.
YOU WILL SEE WOE—
    CHORUS.
—TURN TO GLEE, SO—
    ALL.
—GRIT YOUR TEETH AND SMILE!
SMILE! SMILE! SMILE!

    SNIG. (*clapping his hands to CHORUS*) To work, to work.

(*CHORUS exits as IVY and OLEANDER run in from U.L., step to SNIG. CINDERELLA opens the hamper and checks the contents.*)

    IVY. We can't find the prince anywhere.

OLEANDER. Anyone would think he's hiding.

SNIG. Have you tried the royal gym? He's fond of the trampoline.

IVY & OLEANDER. Which way?

SNIG. (*indicates* U.R.) If you'll follow me. (*SNIG exits* U.R. *IVY and OLEANDER follow.*)

IVY. If he's fond of the trampoline maybe he'll tumble for one of us.

(*IVY and OLEANDER giggle hysterically, exit. Softly humming to herself, CINDERELLA continues her work at the hamper. VLAD sticks his head in from* D.L.)

VLAD. Pssst! You there, serving girl. (*CINDERELLA looks up.*)

CINDERELLA. Me? I?

VLAD. Have they gone?

CINDERELLA. Who?

VLAD. Those husband-hungry girls. (*He steps into view. So the MARRIAGE CANDIDATES won't recognize him, he's in disguise. He's dressed as a chef: white trousers, apron, cook's hat.*) They're causing havoc in the castle.

CINDERELLA. (*back to her work*) Why should that worry you?

VLAD. That's right. I'm not the prince. I only work here. (*to himself*) None of the girls will recognize me in this ingenious disguise.

CINDERELLA. Could you give me a hand with the hamper?

VLAD. Happy to. (*CINDERELLA slams down the lid. VLAD takes one handle (or end), CINDERELLA the other. In doing so, they somehow manage to touch. Only now do they get a good look at one another. They gasp. Freeze. It's love at first sight. NOTE: For added comic effect quickly have the STAGE LIGHTING DIM to a romantic hue — soft pink(s) would work nicely. They stare at each, mesmerized. MUSIC INTROS.*)

THE MOMENT I SAW YOU
(Cinderella, Vlad)

CINDERELLA.
I DON'T KNOW WHAT IT IS
THAT YOU'VE GOT, BUT IT IS
ASTOUNDING

ENOUGH TO MAKE ME SING
LIKE ANYTHING!
HOW ON EARTH DID IT START?
YOU SHOULD HEAR HOW MY HEART
IS POUNDING
BECAUSE YOU TOUCHED MY HAND!
AND
STARS ARE MULTIPLYING
IN MY BRAIN!
THERE IS NO DENYING
I AM FLYING ON A RAINBOW!
I DON'T KNOW WHAT YOU'VE GOT,
BUT I SAY THANKS A LOT
FOR SHARING WHATEVER THIS MAY BE
FLARING IN ME!
    VLAD. (*Seeing she's paused for air, quickly sings* his *part*:)
THERE'S THUNDER
WHEN YOU GLANCE
AT ME! MY DEAR, I WONDER
IF PERCHANCE IT'S ROMANCE?
I CANNOT QUITE EXPLAIN
WHY ALL MY CARES HAVE VANISHED LIKE THE RAIN,
MY DARLING!
NOW WORLDS ARE COLLIDING!
SOULS COINCIDING!
HOW HIGH I'M RIDING,
WHILE SLIDING
RIGHT DOWN A RAINBOW!
BELLS
ALL CHIME ABOVE!
THEIR GOLDEN MUSIC TELLS
ME I'M IN LOVE!
PLEASE TELL ME YOU CAN HEAR THEM TOO!

(*Tricky bit: next* pairs *of lines* (by VLAD/CINDERELLA),
*though written here separately, are sung in interlocking
unison.*)

    CINDERELLA. AND THEIR SUPERHUMAN SONG
SAYS LOVE CAN'T GO WRONG! DARLING!
    VLAD. THEIR SUPERHUMAN SONG
SAYS YOU'LL BE MINE BEFORE LONG! DARLING!

(*Then both go* back *to start of song, and* repeat *darn near every-thing just sung, this time in counterpoint, sliding into coda — overlapping, of course — as with the two couplets just preceding:*)

CINDERELLA.
MY HEART HAS A LOT TO HANDLE!
HOT AS A ROMAN CANDLE!
VLAD.
. . . MUSIC TELLS ME I'M IN LOVE
AND WON'T RECOVER!

(*Final lyrics overlap similarly:*)

CINDERELLA. BUT I FOUND A FEELING LONG-PAST OVERDUE
THE MOMENT I SAW YOU . . . !
VLAD. WHAT A FEELING THRILLED ME THROUGH,
THE MAGICAL MOMENT I OPENED
MY EYES AND SAW YOU . . . !

(*They sigh romantically at each other and exit carrying the hamper/chest between them. IGOR enters* D.R., *followed by GYPOLA.*)

IGOR. Don't bother me. I've got problems of my own.
GYPOLA. All I asked was if you'd seen the prince?
IGOR. Lots of times.
GYPOLA. You must be the worst court jester in the kingdom.
IGOR. I'm the *only* court jester in the kingdom. You're looking at the only game in town.
GYPOLA. You're going to be fired. It's in the cards.
IGOR. If they're your cards they're marked. Their Majesties won't discharge me. (*boasting*) I'm not only a fool, I'm something else.
GYPOLA. You're something else, all right. But what?
IGOR. Never you mind. (*KING and QUEEN enter* D.L.) Ah, there you are, Your Majesties. I must have a word with you. (*hard look to GYPOLA*) In private.
KING. You may leave us, Gypola.
GYPOLA. You're the king. (*She bows, exits.*)
QUEEN. (*to IGOR*) What's up? (*Suddenly, the "barrier" be-*

tween monarchs and subject drops. They speak like conspirators in the dark.)

IGOR. Your Majesties, no one knows you hired me to be Vladimir's keeper. Everyone thinks I'm a joke.

KING. *(to audience)* He said it. I didn't.

QUEEN. We keep up the pretense, don't we?

IGOR. That isn't the point. Those dumdum first ministers, Snig and Snog, didn't look at the calendar.

(As they converse, GYPOLA sneaks in from U.R. and darts behind the thrones. At this locale she can overhear everything. From time to time we see her head appear over the top of one of the thrones as she listens and reacts to the startling *revelations.)*

KING. Calendar? What are you going on about?

IGOR. The ball's tomorrow night and tonight there's a full moon.

KING & QUEEN. *(Aghast) Full moon!*

IGOR. *(checks his watch, speaks to audience)* It'll be here in about ten minutes.

QUEEN. Oh! Oh!

KING. Whatever happens you've got to keep Vlad away from the marriage candidates. The bride mustn't know that he's a wolfman until *after* the wedding.

QUEEN. Or, at least, until her check clears.

IGOR. I know what I'm paid for. *(to audience, boasting)* And it's not to be a fool.

QUEEN. *Nothing* must go wrong.

IGOR. I hear that.

KING. *(angry)* I'll have a word with Snig and Snog.

QUEEN. Those idiots! *(KING and QUEEN march out, D.L. IGOR, playing the role of jester, does a stupid little dance, shaking the bells. GYPOLA steps down to him, arms akimbo.)*

SNOG. So! That's the dark secret of Castle Charming.

IGOR. Gypola!

GYPOLA. *(sly)* Yes, Gypola. Your friendly neighborhood gypsy.

IGOR. *(horrified)* Were you listening!

GYPOLA. No, I was eavesdropping. *(thinking)* Let me think. The last Charming who was cursed to a wolfman's fate was Vladimir's great-grandfather, Fuzzbrain the Seventh.

IGOR. You're not going to tell!

GYPOLA. And lose my commission? Ha!

IGOR. That's a relief.

GYPOLA. Hmmmmmmm.

IGOR. I don't like that sound.

GYPOLA. I've got an idea.

IGOR. I like that even less.

GYPOLA. I know a Weird Museum that would pay a large sum of money for a *stuffed* wolfman.

IGOR. Stuffed wolfman! (*outraged*) I'm going to call the guards!

GYPOLA. This castle doesn't have any. Too expensive.

IGOR. (*forces a smile*) Ha, ha. You're only kidding, aren't you? Ha, ha. Besides, the only way you can kill a werewolf is with a silver bullet. Who has silver bullets these days? (*GYPOLA produces a silver bullet from the folds of her skirt, displays it to the shaken IGOR.*) You do.

GYPOLA. I always follow the gypsy motto — "Be prepared."

IGOR. That's the Boy Scout motto.

GYPOLA. I stole it. (*She pockets bullet. Swift, GYPOLA turns into a menace. With one hand she grabs IGOR's throat and forces him to his knees. She wiggles the fingers of her other hand, mumbo-jumbo, in front of his face, hypnotizing him.*) My eyes . . . look into my eyes.

IGOR. You're trying to hypnotize me.

GYPOLA. I'm not trying to hypnotize you. I'm *doing* it!

IGOR. Stop! Oh! No! Oh! Oh!

GYPOLA. You'll remember nothing of our conversation.

IGOR. Oh! Oh! Oh!

GYPOLA. You're not a court jester and you're not Prince Vladimir's keeper. You're a chicken!

IGOR. Chicken? Me? Never!

GYPOLA. Chicken, chicken, chicken!

IGOR. Never, never, never.

GYPOLA. Chicken, chicken, chicken!

IGOR. Never, never, never, chick, chick, chick. Cheep, cheep, cheep.

(*Hypnotized, poor IGOR imitates a chicken as he darts his head from side to side. Moving like a barnyard fowl, he "kneels or duckwalks" off* D.R. *At the same time, we hear laughter and giggles from offstage,* U.L. *GYPOLA reacts, and not wishing to be seen, swiftly exits* R. *Delighted with having cornered the prince, MARRIAGE CANDIDATES push him* D.S. *VLAD forces himself to smile and be congenial, noblesse oblige. (NOTE: VLAD wears his chef's uniform. No hat, however, or he can wear what he had for his first appearance. Whatever "costume" is preferred it will have to be duplicated for another actor who will shortly make a dramatic appearance.) The MARRIAGE CANDIDATES pull and tug at the hapless young man, each one anxious to catch his eye. (MOTHERS can also be included. Even some female CASTLE STAFF.)*

VLAD. Ladies, please. You're pulling, you're pushing, you're shoving.
MARRIAGE CANDIDATES.
Your Majesty!
Vlad!
You can't escape us!
Finders keepers!
I want the first dance at the Royal Ball.
No, Prince Vladimir, I want the first dance.
I want it!
Me!

(IVY and OLEANDER hurry in from U.R.*)*

IVY. Look, Oleander! There he is!
OLEANDER. The prince!
IVY. A husband! *(They join the melee, VLAD pulls himself free, trying to be as tactful as possible.)*
VLAD. I need air.
IVY & OLEANDER. Give him air, give him air!

(LIGHTING DIMS to signal approaching nightfall. As VLAD speaks he does some "odd" bits of business. He laps his hand, he rubs his ears, he paws the floor with one foot. He growls softly. He scratches. Naturally, the ladies are much too polite to comment on this crude behavior. If the prince wants to lap his hands as if they were paws and scratch as if he had a flea — let him.)

VLAD. Grrrrr. So many beautiful girls! So appealing, so enchanting. Grrrrr. I never realized Vestigia had such a crop of sweets. A box of chocolates, that's what you are. Yum, yum. (*MARRIAGE CANDIDATES giggle.*)

MARRIAGE CANDIDATES.
Oh, you're a poet!
How lovely!
I may swoon, or faint, or something!
I love poets.
He thinks we're sweet. Oooooo . . .

IVY. Oh, don't stop.
OLEANDER. Tell us more.
GIRL #1. Tell us what you're thinking.
GIRL #2. Tell us your every thought.
GIRL #3. We're hungry for every word.

VLAD. *You're* hungry? (*showing his teeth, a wolfish grin*) What about me?

(*MUSIC INTROS, VLAD, LADIES sing:*)

THIS IS MY NIGHT TO HOWL

VLAD.
LOOK AT THIS MENU OF YUMMY YOUNG GIRLS!

(*NOTE: Until the transformation-moment, the LADIES think this and similar lines are just romantic* metaphors, *so they remain bright and cheery until the wolfman appears. The moon is coming up momentarily, and the pre-appearance "vibes" are warping VLAD's mind and words.*)

LADIES.
DELICIOUS!
VLAD.
I AM PLEASED AS A PUP!
LADIES.
INSPECT ME!
VLAD.
SOME RUDDY, SOME PASTY —   .
I MUSTN'T BE HASTY —
ALL LOOKING SO TASTY —
I COULD EAT YOU UP!
LOOK NOW AS BEAUTY ABUNDANT UNFURLS!

LADIES.
GRANT OUR WISHES!
    VLAD.
NARY A FROWN OR A SCOWL!
    LADIES.
SELECT ME!
    VLAD.
IT'S SUCH A DELIGHT TO
HAVE MARRIAGE TO PLIGHT YOU!
IT'S TRULY MY NIGHT TO HOWL!
    LADIES.
WE SEEM TO BE
QUITE A SENSATION!
NEVER HAVE WE
ENGENDERED SO MUCH SALIVATION!

(*A few lightning-flickers in sky, now (no* thunder *yet.*)

    VLAD.
THOUGH THEY SAY BEAUTY IS ONLY
    SKIN-DEEP . . .
    LADIES.
WHAT OF IT?!
    VLAD.
. . . THAT'S DEEP ENOUGH FOR ROMANCE!
    LADIES.
HOW YUMMY!
    VLAD.
I'M WILLING TO TRY IT!
LET CALORIES RIOT!
DON'T BOTHER TO DIET!
FAT GIRLS HAVE A CHANCE!
    LADIES. (*Delighted; especially the plumper candidates*)
HOW NICE TO KNOW WE CAN LET OUR FLESH
    CREEP . . .
    VLAD.
HOW I LOVE IT!
    LADIES.
. . . OVER BOTH BELLY AND JOWL!
    VLAD.
AND TUMMY!

LADIES.
FAT LADIES ARE LOYAL!
THEY'D NEVER RECOIL (sung as "re-coy-al")
FROM HEARING HIS ROYAL GROWL!
VLAD. (*at foot of throne-dias, now, starts backing up steps*)
DEAR LADIES, JUST LEND ME YOUR EAR!
LADIES.
OH JOY!
VLAD. (*will back up stairs till between both thrones*)
THE MOON SOON WILL APPEAR . . .
LADIES.
OH, BOY!
VLAD. (*as full moon starts to rise into view in open casement above throne*)
. . . AND YOU'RE GOING TO HEAR . . .
LADIES.
STOP DELAYING . . .
VLAD. (*springs up so he now has one foot upon each throne (or throne-arm)*)
. . . ME . . .
LADIES.
. . . AND START THAT HAPPY BAYING!
VLAD.
. . . HOWL!
LADIES. (*joyously*)
ME, TOO!
VLAD/LADIES.
OW-WOOOO . . . !

(*THUNDERCLAP and BLACKOUT, MUSIC continuing for three bars in darkness, and then LIGHTS COME UP and the WOLFMAN now stands on thrones where VLAD just was; LADIES are no longer either cheery or delighted. They're terrified!*)

LADIES. (*shriek in terror as WOLFMAN springs down, starts pursuing them here, there, and everywhere*) Aaaaaah . . . !

(*MUSIC has turned weird the moment lights come up, and now CURTAIN starts as weird music intensifies, and WOLF-MAN and LADIES gallop all over the place. In a burst for freedom WOLFMAN leaps into the wings, L. GYPOLA with a rifle to her shoulder, appears* R., *and taking aim, stalks after him. At the moment MUSIC ENDS:)*

Curtain is down

End of ACT ONE

ACT TWO

Scene 1

Setting: *Same as Act One.*

At Rise: The following morning. IVY, OLEANDER and MRS. SHRUB enter U.L. and move C. They're excited.

Ivy. The whole castle's talking about it.

Oleander. The whole countryside.

Mrs. Shrub. Imagine! A beast in the castle. Whoever could have let it in?

Ivy. One minute the prince is standing here and the next minute he's gone. Replaced by "the thing."

Mrs. Shrub. Vestigia does have strange neighbors. Those Draculas are always up to something nasty. As for the Frankensteins — well, the less said about them the better. The last time I had Baron Frankenstein for dinner he took home all the bones.

Ivy. What's so odd about that?

Mrs. Shrub. He doesn't have a dog.

Oleander. I was hoping the wolf would scare away the marriage candidates.

Ivy. All but us. (*IVY and OLEANDER giggle.*)

Mrs. Shrub. Good gracious! You don't suppose the creature devoured the prince?

Oleander. No, Mama. We saw him walking in the garden early this morning. He was feeding the pigeons.

Mrs. Shrub. (*out to audience*) What a mystery.

(*CINDERELLA enters L. She carries a ballgown in her arms.*)

Cinderella. (*curtsies*) Good morning, Ivy, good morning, Oleander.

Ivy & Oleander. (*indifferent*) 'Morning.

Mrs. Shrub. Oh, it's you, uh, er — (*to IVY*) What's her name again?

Ivy & Oleander. Cinderella.

Cinderella. (*to MRS. SHRUB*) Your stepdaughter.

Ivy. Don't tell anyone we're related.

Oleander. We don't want anyone to know.

CINDERELLA. (*hurt*) I'll remember.

IVY. You missed all the excitement last night, Cinderella.

CINDERELLA. I did?

OLEANDER. A furry beast got into the castle.

CINDERELLA. (*calmly*) I saw it.

OTHERS. (*amazed*) You saw it?

CINDERELLA. I was in the passageway that leads to the garden scrubbing the floor. (*to audience*) It hadn't been scrubbed in months. I know dirt when I see it.

MRS. SHRUB. Go on.

CINDERELLA. It ran toward me — and skidded to a stop.

OTHERS. Skidded to a stop?

CINDERELLA. It looked at me and, then, dashed away.

IVY. Weren't you frightened?

CINDERELLA. I wasn't frightened. It had kind eyes.

OTHERS. Kind eyes? A wolf? Ha, ha, ha, ha, ha!

IVY. Silly girl.

OLEANDER. Silly, silly Cinderella.

CINDERELLA. (*mustering a gentle defense*) Father always said I was intelligent.

MRS. SHRUB. Your father was a dreamer. He had no right to go up in that balloon and leave me alone. Anyone would think he was trying to get away from me. Boo-hoo. Ah, well, he's gone and we're here. Life must go on. What did you want, uh, er —

CINDERELLA. Cinderella.

MRS. SHRUB. Whatever.

CINDERELLA. If you're going to wear this gown to the ball I will have to let out the waist.

MRS. SHRUB. What are you talking about, you wretch? I have the smallest waist in the kingdom — everyone knows that. If I swallow a gumdrop it shows. (*IVY and OLEANDER cover their mouths with their hands and giggle at this fib.*) Mind you, see that my beautiful daughters look brilliant for the ball. Now, get out of here and get to work, you lazy creature.

CINDERELLA. (*sadly*) Yes, Stepmother.

(*CINDERELLA exits* L. *as IGOR, still in his chicken state, enters from* R.)

IGOR. Cheep, cheep, cheep, cheep, cheep, cheep.

IVY. Look, Oleander. It's the fool.

OLEANDER. I think he's cute. You married?

MRS. SHRUB. Oleander! (*IGOR straightens up, back to himself.*)

IGOR. Wow! What happened to me? I can't remember a thing.

IVY. Maybe the wolf bit you. (*Females laugh.*)

IGOR. (*wide-eyed*) *Wolf!*

IVY. Last night. It chased everyone in the castle.

OLEANDER. I wonder if that wolf's married.

MRS. SHRUB. Forget the wolf. Come along, my lovelies, a morning walk will put color in your cheeks.

IVY & OLEANDER. Yes, Mama. (*MRS. SHRUB, IVY, OLEANDER heads high, exit* U.R.)

IGOR. (*to audience*) Drat! He turned into a wolf when I wasn't looking. Their Majesties aren't going to like this. Igor, you're in *big* trouble.

(*Suddenly, noise of great commotion, from* D.L. *and SNIG, SNOG, MALE STAFF back in holding off a mob of angry PEASANTS, who are led by an irate FARMER. They carry pitchforks, etc. NOTE: See FLEXIBLE CASTING. The PEASANTS, for example, can be the MARRIAGE CANDI-DATES and MOTHERS dressed as rustics (even as males), with scarves over their heads. Or, if you're utilizing a large cast, CHORUS MEMBERS. They move* C.)

SNIG. No, no, no. You're mistaken.

FARMER. Mistaken? I know what I saw. *It was a wolf!*

SNOG. Nonsense.

FARMER. Sharp teeth, sharp claws.

PEASANTS. A wolf! It was a wolf!

SNOG. (*to IGOR*) You fool! (*IGOR cringes.*)

IGOR. That's me.

FARMER. I say it was the prince.

IGOR. Impossible!

FARMER. The Charming curse. The last one who had it was Fuzzbrain the Fourth.

SNIG. Fifth.

SNOG. Sixth.

IGOR. Seventh and that makes bingo!

SNIG. You're imagining things.

SNOG. Peasants are always imagining things.

PEASANTS.
No!

We know what we saw!

A wolf!

FARMER. It was a *royal* wolf. Beneath the fur I recognized Vlad, the prince.

SNIG. You'll be sued for slander.

SNOG. Defamation of character.

IGOR. My attorney will call on you in the morning.

FARMER. A wolf creature!

SNOG. Enough!

FARMER. A wolfman, a dog animal, a werewolf!

IGOR. We get the general idea. (*to SNIG*) Make him stop. He's making me nervous.

FARMER. It scared the cows and frightened the sheep. The cows won't give milk and the sheep have lost their wool.

IGOR. How much wool?

FARMER. Three bags full.

IGOR. Baa-baa, baa-baa.

(*In the following, PALACE refers to IGOR, SNIG, SNOG, MALE STAFF. FARMER and OTHERS = PEASANTRY. The PEASANTRY lyrics are in brackets. MUSIC INTROS. They sing:*)

IT WAS A WOLF!

PALACE/(PEASANTRY).

YOU'RE MUCH MISTAKEN, SURELY COMMON SENSE DECREES!

(IT WAS A WOLF!)

YOU'RE MERELY JUMPING TO A SILLY CONCLUSION!

(IT WAS A WOLF!)

THE HOWLING CANDIDATES CREATED CONFUSION!

(IT WAS A WOLF!)

THE CREEPING SHADOWS MERELY CAUSED AN ILLUSION!

BOTH.

KINDLY MAKE NO MISTAKE! WE KNOW WHAT IS WHAT!

PALACE/(PEASANTRY).

(IT WAS A WOLF! WE SAW IT!)

YOU'RE FINDING FIRE THAT YOU HAVEN'T THE

46   CINDERELLA MEETS THE WOLFMAN

SMOKE FOR!
(IT WAS A WOLF! WE SAW IT!)
EVENTS WERE NORMAL! DON'T YOU TRY TO EVOKE
  MORE!
(IT WAS A WOLF! WE SAW IT!)
A PRINCE DOES NOT BECOME A CREATURE OF
  FOLKLORE!
  Both.
SURELY YOU KNOW IT'S TRUE! FACTS ARE FACTS!
  Palace/(Peasantry).
SOME NIGHTS
(IN THE MIST . . .)
THINGS MAY MISUNDERSTOOD BE!
(. . . EVENTS ILLUMINE!)
BY RIGHTS,
(WE INSIST . . .)
YOU SHOULD LAUGH THEM AWAY!
(. . . WE KNOW WHAT WE'RE SAYING!)
THE LIGHTS
(THINGS EXIST . . .)
WEREN'T BRIGHT AS THEY SHOULD BE!
(. . . THAT AIN'T QUITE HUMAN!)
INSANE SUPPOSITIONS! WEATHER CONDITIONS!
(OH! WE FEAR . . .)
SHEER SUPERSTITIONS! STUFF AND NONSENSE!
(. . . THAT WOE DRAWS NEAR!)

YOU CAN'T CONVINCE US TO ESCHEW OUR
  FACULTIES!
(IT WAS A WOLF!)
·WHEN BLOOD IS NOBLE, THERE'S NO REASON TO
  WORRY!
(IT WAS A WOLF!)
A PRINCE MAY SKULK A BIT, BUT NEVER WILL
  SCURRY!
(IT WAS A WOLF!)
A ROYAL PERSON'S MUCH TOO FINE TO GROW
  FURRY!
  Both.
NOT A WORD HAVE YOU HEARD! YOU ARE IN A RUT!
  Palace/(Peasantry).
(IT WAS A WOLF! WE SWEAR IT!)

OH, STOP INSISTING ON HIS HYBRIDIZATION!
(IT WAS A WOLF! WE SWEAR IT!)
WE CANNOT CREDIT SUCH A MANIFESTATION!
(IT WAS A WOLF! WE SWEAR IT!)
WE'RE GETTING NOWHERE IN OUR ARGUMEN-
TATION!
    BOTH.
WHAT THE DEUCE! WHAT'S THE USE!
    PALACE/(PEASANTRY).
MUST WE ARGUE?!
(VLADIMIR IS THE GUY!)
WE ARE TRULY FAR TOO
(WHY TRY . . .)
HARD TO CONVINCE!
(. . . STOPPING
US FROM DROPPING . . .)
IT'S CLEAR
THAT ONLY SHEER
INSANITY. . .
    BOTH.
. . . HINTS
THAT IT WAS THE PRINCE!

(*SNIG and SNOG, IGOR, STAFF dialogue overlapping, push FARMER and PEASANTRY out,* L.)

    PALACE. Get out!
Out, out!
Move along!
Stupid peasants!
Stupid story!
    PEASANTRY.
Wolf!
We know what we saw!
You can't do this to us!
Stop pushing!
It was a wolf!

(*As the PEASANTRY is shoved from view— Enter* R. *PAULA POND,* fabulous *Hollywood movie star!!! PAULA is dressed in* glamorous *fashion. Beautifully made up. Her coiffure is perfection. Jewelry sparkles everywhere on her person.* She lights up the stage. *She's successful, she's tough, she's famous, she's smart, she's vain — but she has a good heart. She parades* C. *and spins around as if she were modelling her clothes, hopes to catch the attention of PALACE who, at last, have managed to get rid of the PEASANTRY.*)

PAULA. (*strikes a pose*) Paula Pond has arrived in Vestigia . . . no applause, please. (*no reaction*) Paula Pond is here. (*PALACE members turn.*)
PALACE. Who? (*PAULA can't believe their reaction.*) Who?

(*NOTE: If there aren't enough male chorus actors, use SNIG, SNOG and IGOR to fill out the ranks . . . RODOLPHO, too. MITZI, PAULA's maid, enters* D.R., *indicates her employer with a hand gesture.*)

MITZI. (*announces*) Hollywood's number one box office sensation — *Miss Paula Pond!* (*MITZI is petite, winsome and all smiles.*)
PALACE. Who?
PAULA. (*modestly*) No applause, please.

(*RODOLPHO, PAULA's liveried chauffeur, enters* D.R., *stands beside MITZI, gestures to the star.*)

RODOLPHO. Broadway's reigning queen and star of Forty-First, Forty-Second, Forty-Third, Forty-Fourth *and* Forty-Fifth Street!!!
PAULA. (*modestly*) No applause, please. (*Realizing a great person has arrived, PALACE begins to applaud.*) Thank you, thank you. You shouldn't.
SNIG. In the confusion of things I forgot you were arriving.
PAULA. I don't usually accept invitations from folks I don't know, but Vestigia sounded so interesting. "Smallest little kingdom in the world." (*SNOG sidles up to SNIG, whispers.*)
SNOG. I don't get it.
SNIG. (*stage whisper*) I mailed out invitations to famous people and she's the only one who showed up.
SNOG. She'll be great for publicity. (*shoves SNIG toward PAULA*) Go for it.
SNIG. I'm Snig, the First First Minister. (*nods to SNOG*) He's Snog, the Second First Minister.

PAULA. Hi, guys. (*to MITZI and RODOLPHO*) A royal ball. It's like something out of a fairy tale. (*introduces*) This is my personal maid, Mitzi.

MITZI. Hello.

PAULA. My chauffeur, Rodolpho. I call him Rudy for short. (*RODOLPHO clicks his heels together, Prussian style, gives a curt nod of the head.*) Don't you just love the way he does that? I love his name, too. Rodolpho. It means "famous wolf."

PALACE. Auuuugh! (*They quickly recover.*)

PAULA. Did I say something wrong?

SNIG. No, no, no.

IGOR. (*moves in*) Welcome to Castle Charming.

PAULA. (*startled*) Eeek! I didn't see you there.

IGOR. I'm Igor.

PAULA. (*to SNIG*) Gore is right.

SNIG. I hope you won't be intimidated at the thought of meeting royalty.

PAULA. *Moi?* You've got to be kidding.

(*MUSIC INTROS. MITZI exits* D.R., *so PAULA is left onstage surrounded by men. She sings:*)

HOLLYWOOD ROYALTY

PAULA.
TO BOW AND SCRAPE I FIND A BIT EXCESSIVE.
NOBILITY WILL NEVER TOP THE ARTS.
SO THE ONLY "TITLES" THAT I FIND IMPRESSIVE
ARE THOSE LOVELY OP'NING CREDITS
WHEN A MOTION PICTURE STARTS!

GIVE . . . ME . . . A . . . PART
THAT WINS YOUR HEART,
AND YOU CAN KEEP THOSE BARONS AND EARLS!
AN ELEGANT CHASSIS
BEATS HAILE SELASSIE!
THE WORLD LOVES BEAUTIFUL GIRLS!

PAULA (MEN). (*She and they will begin to stroll-strut a bit at first, as all sing, but soon blossom into full-scale one-girl-plus-multiple-males-dance-number, probably ending with her seated*

*jauntily atop a veritable pyramid of adoring men at song's
climax.)*
ALTHOUGH A CROWN
(A KINGLY CROWN!)
CAN BRING RENOWN,
(ALL OVER TOWN!)
THAT'S NOT THE ONLY PATHWAY TO FAME!
(WAY TO FAME!)
    ALL.
I (WE) REALLY REJOICE THAT,
WHEN GIVEN THE CHOICE, THAT
OLD WORLD WANTS A BEAUTIFUL DAME!
    PAULA.
THOUGH KINGS AND QUEENS ARE WORSHIPPED
BY FAWNING PALACE STAFFS,
    ALL.
THEY NEVER WILL
ENJOY THE THRILL
OF SIGNING AUTOGRAPHS!
    PAULA (MEN).
WHEN YOU ASSESS
(FOR MORE OR LESS!)
A MARCHIONESS,
(WHO'S NOT A MESS!)
ALTHOUGH YOU MAY BE PROPERLY AWED,
(AND APPLAUD!)
    ALL.
HER VIEW-FROM-THE-TOP CORN
WON'T SELL ANY POPCORN!
THE WORLD WANTS A BEAUTIFUL BROAD!
    PAULA.
WHY SHOULD I SHAKE WHEN SUMMONED
TO MEET WITH ROYALTY?
    ALL.
IT SIMPLY MEANS
THE KINGS AND QUEENS
ARE LONGING TO MEET ME (SHE)!
    PAULA (MEN).
TO ME, NOBLESSE (THAT OLD NOBLESSE!)
COULD NOT MEAN LESS! (WHO NEEDS LARGESSE?!)
SO LET THEM KEEP THEIR CRUMPETS AND TEA!
(NOT FOR SHE!)

TO ME, WHEN ADORING
HEADWAITERS ARE POURING
CHAMPAGNE
IT IS PLAIN
AS CAN BE
(TO SEE)
THAT
    ALL.
THE WORLD FINDS ROYALTY
IN BEAUTIFUL . . .
    PAULA (MEN).
. . . ME!
(GLAMOROUS HOLLYWOOD ROYALTY
IS SHE!)

SNIG. (*to OTHERS, clapping his hands*) We must prepare for the ball. (*OTHERS exit. To PAULA:*) I will see to your rooms.

PAULA. Thanks, Snog.

SNIG. Snig. (*He exits.*)

PAULA. (*to RODOLPHO*) Snig? Snog? They sound like something left over from the Snow White and the Seven Dwarfs.

RODOLPHO. This country isn't even on the map.

PAULA. I'll put it on the map. You have no spirit of adventure, Rudy. Anyone can go to a party in Paris or Rome or London. But I'm not anyone. I'm Paula Pond.

RODOLPHO. (*starts to recite again*) Star of Forty-First, Forty-Second, Forty-Third, Forty-Fourth — (*PAULA cuts him off with an upraised hand. CINDERELLA, carrying two buckets (supposedly filled with water) struggles in. PAULA sees her.*)

PAULA. Don't just stand there. Can't you see the girl needs help? Give the child a hand. (*RODOLPHO crosses for CINDERELLA.*)

RODOLPHO. I'll take those, miss.

CINDERELLA. No, no, sir. I couldn't allow that. I'm used to hard work. Mopping and scrubbing is my destiny.

PAULA. What's your name, child?

CINDERELLA. (*curtsies*) My name is Cinderella and I am "the fastest veggie-chopper in Vestigia." (*PAULA and RODOLPHO don't know what to make of this.*)

PAULA. (*long pause*) Well, it's good to be good at something. (*to RODOLPHO*) See what's keeping Mitzi with the luggage?

RODOLPHO. (*exits, mumbling*) Fastest veggie-chopper in Vestigia . . . (*CINDERELLA puts down the water buckets. Awed by this latest arrival to Castle Charming.*)

CINDERELLA. What a beautiful lady you are.

PAULA. Naturally. I'm a Hollywood star.

CINDERELLA. (*sighs*) Like a fairy godmother.

PAULA. If you say so. Tell me, kid, since you work here — what's this prince like?

CINDERELLA. Vlad? Prince Vladimir?

PAULA. If he's the one who's getting married.

CINDERELLA. I've never met him. I've never seen him. You forget, miss, I occupy a low station in life.

PAULA. (*to audience*) Strange girl. (*to CINDERELLA*) Who is this Vladimir tying the knot with?

CINDERELLA. Pardon?

PAULA. Who's the ball and chain?

CINDERELLA. I don't understand.

PAULA. Who is the prince marrying?

CINDERELLA. No one knows. He'll make the announcement tonight. After the final dance.

(*MRS. SHRUB, IVY and OLEANDER enter from u.l.*)

MRS. SHRUB. Hurry, girls. You must take a nap and have your hair done.

IVY & OLEANDER. Yes, Mama.

MRS. SHRUB. (*to CINDERELLA*) You there, whatever your name is. Why are you wasting time? Your stepsisters must get ready for the ball.

IVY. Polish my shoes, Cinderella.

OLEANDER. Press my gown, Cinderella.

MRS. SHRUB. When you're done dressing hair and polishing shoes and pressing gowns, you can give me a manicure, pedicure, and massage.

PAULA. (*to audience*) I'd like to give her a kick.

IVY. Don't you wish you were going to the ball, Cinderella? Ha, ha.

OLEANDER. Imagine the prince paying attention to a penniless kitchen slavey with smudge on her face and soot on her dress. Ha, ha.

MRS. SHRUB. Tonight's the night.

IVY & OLEANDER. I'm going to be a princess . . . I'm going

to be a princess. (*They're out. CINDERELLA sees that PAULA is staring at her, forces a smile.*)

CINDERELLA. That's my stepmother Mrs. Shrub. And my stepsisters Ivy and Oleander. They're really not as mean as they sound.

PAULA. You're too good to be true, kid.

CINDERELLA. (*blinks her eyelashes out to audience*) I know.

PAULA. But you don't fool old Paula Pond. I've been around. I can tell you'd give anything to go to the ball. And why not? The prince might smile in your direction. You wouldn't be half bad if you washed your face.

CINDERELLA. The prince smile at me? (*displays her rags*) In a soot-colored gown of dishrags?

(*RODOLPHO and MITZI enter* R. *with PAULA's handsome luggage; jewel case, hat box, etc. They start to cross* L.)

PAULA. Hold it, Mitzi, Rudy. (*They stop. PAULA steps to bench,* S.R., *bench and moves it so that it faces out to audience. She motions to CINDERELLA.*) Okay, Cinderella. (*points to bench*) Park it.

CINDERELLA. But my water buckets . . .

PAULA. Dry up. (*Nervously, CINDERELLA crosses to the bench, sits.*) When I get done with you, you won't know yourself.

CINDERELLA. Is that good?

MITZI. Couldn't be any worse.

(*PAULA signals MITZI and RODOLPHO to put down and open the luggage. NOTE: PAULA is attempting to see what will look best on CINDERELLA, so what they produce will not be what the actress will actually wear at the ball. Once song begins, PAULA puts a gown over the rags, adds bracelets, tries a tiara, hands CINDERELLA some gloves, a hand mirror, etc. MITZI and RODOLPHO assist, convinced they are working wonders. CINDERELLA is lost in a swirl of "possibility." MUSIC INTROS. PAULA sings:*)

MAGIC TIME

PAULA.
IT'S MAGIC TIME!
A BALL'S NOT NECESSARILY A TRAGIC TIME

OF YOUR LIFE!

RODOLPHO/MITZI.
JUST REMEMBER:
HOLLYWOOD FINALES ARE THE PRODUCT OF
  ILLUSION!
FOR A GREAT CONCLUSION
ONE HAS TO CAST A SPELL!

PAULA.
IF THE PRINCE
IS GONNA FALL IN LOVE WITH YOU, YOU MUST
  EVINCE
A RARE CHARM! DISARM HIM BY MY MAGICAL
  ASSIST,
AND IN HIS ARMS YOU'LL SOON BE KISSED!

PAULA/RODOLPHO/MITZI.
ENLIST
THE AID OF ONE WHO KNOWS
EXTRAORDINARY CLOTHES
AND BECKONING PERFUME
DRAW MEN TO THEIR DOOM!
TAKE A TIP AND TRUST US!
LET US DO YOU JUSTICE!
(*Since they are garbing and attempting to prettify her
throughout song, this is the point for a fashion-wig:*)
IN THESE GOLDEN CURLS
YOU'LL MAKE OTHER GIRLS
SOON DECAY AWAY!

CINDERELLA. (*afraid to believe her good fortune*)
CAN IT BE?
AM I GLAMOROUSLY
ALARMING?

TRIO.
WE
GUARANTEE
YOU WILL STUN PRINCE CHARMING!

RODOLPHO/MITZI.
YOUR STRANGE EXOTIC ALLURE
IS TOO HOT TO ENDURE!
WE'RE SURE
THE PRINCE WILL BE MINCEMEAT!

CINDERELLA.
I'VE
NEVER FELT SO ALIVE

AND THRIVING!

TRIO.
THAT'S YOUR INHERENT *PANACHE*
REVIVING!

CINDERELLA.
HOW CAN I THANK YOU?

PAULA.
THERE'S NO NEED OF THAT!

TRIO.
ALL WE'VE DONE
IS SHARE THE FUN
OF . . .

ALL.
MAGIC TIME!

CINDERELLA.
THIS SEX-APPEAL IS SUCH A HANDY GADGET, I'M
IN A SPIN!

TRIO.
KEEP YOUR CHIN UP!
WHEN IT COMES TO STEALING HEARTS,
YOU'RE BOUND TO BE A ROBBER
GUARANTEED TO CLOBBER
EACH GUY
WHO MEETS YOUR EYE!

PAULA.
AT THE BALL
THE SIGHT OF YOU IS GONNA STAGGER ALL
WHO ATTEND! YOU'LL RENDER

TRUE BLUE SEX-APPEAL SUBLIME,
AND ONCE HIS WAYS YOU'RE TAMING . . .

TRIO.
. . . YOU'LL SPEND YOUR DAYS ACCLAIMING . . .

CINDERELLA.
. . . THE BLINDING BLAZE OF MAGIC TIME!

TRIO.
RON-TATA-TAH FOR MAGIC TIME! MAGIC TIME!

(*At the conclusion of "Magic Time" CINDERELLA is
"dressed." She stands, looking at her dirty face in the hand
mirror. The wig doesn't fit. The tiara is off to one side. The
gown is much too big (or too small). The gloves don't fit and
she can barely stand in her new shoes. A graceless misfit.*)

CINDERELLA looks like a grade-A klutz!!! MITZI, RO-DOLPHO, PAULA frown at their efforts.)

MITZI. She didn't come out right.

RODOLPHO. We must have done something wrong. (*Nonetheless CINDERELLA is enchanted with herself, continues to stare at her reflection in the hand mirror.*)

CINDERELLA. I am — beautiful.

MITZI & RODOLPHO. Huh?

CINDERELLA. If only that palace chef could see me now.

PAULA. We can do better. *Much* better.

MITZI. She has such tiny feet.

PAULA. (*looks*) So you do.

RODOLPHO. How about that little pair you picked up at the Rodeo Drive garage sale?

PAULA. They'd be perfect. They look just like glass. (*to CINDERELLA*) I was going to use them for planters.

(*She signals MITZI and RODOLPHO to pack up. QUEEN flutters in, L., delighted that a "name" has turned up for the ball.*)

QUEEN. Miss Pond, Snig told me you were here. I am Queen Charming. Welcome, welcome to Vestigia.

PAULA. Catch you later, Queenie. I got things to do. This is going to take some time. (*She grabs CINDERELLA by the wrist and pulls her offstage. With the luggage, MITZI and RODOLPHO follow.*)

QUEEN. But, er, Miss Pond? Miss Pond, where are you going?

(*KING enters L.*)

KING. I am King Charming. Welcome to Vestigia — smallest little kingdom in the world.

QUEEN. Save your breath. She's gone.

KING. Where?

QUEEN. Your guess is as good as mine.

KING. I hope she's not leaving the kingdom. I want to take some publicity pictures.

QUEEN. We have more important things to worry about.

KING. I wish you hadn't said that. I presume you're referring to last evening?

QUEEN. Wait until I get my hands on that Igor.

(On cue, IGOR skips in from D.R., *in a merry mood. He's delighted with the arrival of PAULA POND, more-or-less sings:)*

IGOR. "THE WORLD FINDS ROYALTY
IN BEAUTIFUL . . .
. . . ME!
GLAMOROUS HOLLYWOOD ROYALTY IS ME . . . "

QUEEN. *(steps to him)* You villain.

IGOR. I've always wanted to go to Hollywood and see the stars, Your Majesties.

QUEEN. I'll show you stars. *(QUEEN takes the stick with the bells and bops him on the head.)*

IGOR. Ow!

KING. You were supposed to watch the prince.

IGOR. I know. I can't understand it. I can't remember a thing about last night.

KING. The palace staff has denied everything. Whatever happens nothing must go wrong until the wedding.

IGOR. I'll watch myself.

QUEEN. You'll watch the prince.

KING. That's what you're paid for.

IGOR. Your Majesties forget. I haven't been paid in over three years.

QUEEN. And you're not worth a penny of it.

KING. We can't waste any more time talking to this fool. *(He offers QUEEN his hand. She takes it. They start to exit. QUEEN stops, turns back to IGOR.)*

QUEEN. The royal guillotine hasn't been used in centuries. However . . . if you foul up one more time — chop. *(Horrified, IGOR grabs his throat.)*

IGOR. Chop?

QUEEN & KING. Chop, chop. *(They exit.)*

IGOR. Oh! Oh! This isn't one of my days. The guillotine? Chop, chop.

(GYPOLA enters D.R., *dragging the rifle behind her.)*

GYPOLA. I missed him.

IGOR. Who?

GYPOLA. *(lies)* I was hunting a squirrel last night.

IGOR. (*thinking hard*) Hmmmm. I'm trying to remember something and it has to do with you.

GYPOLA. You don't know what you're talking about.

IGOR. (*perplexed*) I look at you and I think chicken.

GYPOLA. Watch it.

IGOR. Did you hypnotize me?

GYPOLA. A gypsy can only hypnotize someone who has a weak mind.

IGOR. That lets me out.

GYPOLA. Tell me something, Igor.

IGOR. Shoot. (*realizes she's holding a rifle*) Forget I said that.

GYPOLA. The "Charming Curse." When it stuck old Fuzz-brain the Eighth —

IGOR. — Seventh —

GYPOLA. How long did it last?

IGOR. Until the full moon was on the wane.

GYPOLA. In other words, it lingered for a few days.

IGOR. It's only a legend. Why do you ask?

GYPOLA. (*out to audience*) I want another shot — and this time I won't miss.

*End of ACT TWO, Scene One**

SCENE 2

SETTING: The Royal Ball.

AT RISE: Couples are dancing to an overly-languid tempo. IVY with SNIG, OLEANDER with SNOG, IGOR with GYPOLA (minus her rifle, of course). Since the neighbors are the Dra-culas and the Frankensteins we might see the Frankenstein MONSTER (a face mask works nicely) and a VAMPIRE — MITZI and RODOLPHO could enact these characters. As the dancers do their thing, KING and QUEEN will enter and take their places on the thrones.

---

*Scene break is indicated for the sole purpose of marking a passage in time. From day to night. No curtain. A shift in the STAGE LIGHTING does the trick. GYPOLA and IGOR move to the side (strike water buckets, reposition bench) and we're ready for the big night as ENSEMBLE moves into view and MUSIC INTROS.

LOVELY PEOPLE, LOVELY WALTZ

COUPLES. (*singing wearily and* much *too slowly*)
LOVELY PEOPLE IN A LOVELY WALTZ,
THROBBING PULSES DOING SOMERSAULTS
AS WITH THE MUSIC WE'RE SLOWLY SWEPT AWAY,
CAPTURING ENRAPTURING DELIGHTS WHERE WE
 MAY!
 NOW THE WALTZ ACCELERATES THE BEAT!
(*It does so, now becoming slowly a bright, perky dance.*)
IT GETS HARDER STAYING ON YOUR FEET!
TOES DISENCHANTED BY PAIN AS YOU DANCE
ARE SHRIEKING YOU
SHOULD SEEK A NEW
ROMANCE!
THEN . . .
 FEMALES.
LADIES, REMEMBER THAT TO SHOW YOUR PAIN
(*NOTE*: *They rub their dancing shoes to emphasize bruised and
weary feet.*)
MEANS YOU WON'T BE REIGN-
ING UP THERE ON THE THRONE!
SO GRIT YOUR PRETTY TEETH!
PRETEND YOU'RE CAREFREE!
DON'T YEARN FOR BARE FEET
OR YOU'LL BE LEFT ALONE!
 MALES.
WHAT ARE WE DOING HERE CAVORTING
WHEN IT'S VERY CLEAR
THAT OUR MANLY PRESENCE HERE IS SUPERFLUOUS!
YES, WE ARE HANDSOME MEN,
BUT WHAT'S THE POINT OF HANDSOME WHEN
HE'S NOT SEEKING GENTLEMEN,
AND SURE WON'T PICK US!
 ALL.
BUT IF WE'RE NOT SELECTED,
THERE'S YUMMY FOOD AT THE BUFFET,
SO IF WE'RE NEGLECTED,
WE'LL TRY TO EAT OUR BLUES AWAY!
DON'T BE DEJECTED,
JUST NIBBLE ON A *CANAPÉ*
.

AND, IF YOUR SPIRITS SAG,
TAKE A DOGGY-BAG
HOME! KEEP SMILING

AS YOU STRIVE TO LOOK YOUR VERY BEST!
LET'S CONTRIVE TO PASS THE ROYAL TEST!
BUT IF WE DON'T, TO THE PHONE BOOK WE'LL
    CRAWL!
LET'S HOPE IT LISTS
PODIATRISTS
WHO'LL MAKE A HOUSE-CALL,
ONCE WE'VE LEFT THIS MAD
PRINCE VLAD-
IMIR'S BALL!

(*KING and QUEEN applaud dutifully.*)

> KING. Delightful, delightful.
> QUEEN. Charming, charming. (*ENSEMBLE bows, curtsies.*)
> ENSEMBLE. *Your Majesties.*

(*As soon as the dance ends, SNOG moves* U.S. *to stand beside the
    KING's throne. He takes a large staff from behind the dais.
    He is now the majordomo.*)

> QUEEN. It is our firm wish that you all enjoy yourselves on this
night of nights. The buffet will be ready shortly.
> IGOR. What are we having?
> KING. We're having sushi.
> ENSEMBLE. (*pleased*) *Sushi!* (*They applaud the prospect.*)

(*From offstage,* U.L. *we hear the cackle of MRS. SHRUB.*)

> MRS. SHRUB. (*offstage*) *Here I am!!! Better late than never!*
> SNOG. (*bangs staff on floor*: BANG! BANG! BANG!) Mrs.
Walter Shrub, richest widow in Vestigia!
> IVY & OLEANDER. It's Mama!

(*MRS. SHRUB ENTERS, overdressed and foolish-looking.*)

> MRS. SHRUB. (*curtsies*) I would have been here sooner, Your

Majesties, but my stupid servant couldn't be found. I had to dress myself.

IGOR. (*to audience*) Obviously in the dark. (*MRS. SHRUB moves from one guest to another, shaking hands, curtsying, ad libbing sub rosa chit-chat. SNOG, again, bangs the staff: BANG! BANG! BANG!*)

SNOG. Miss Paula Pond — star of Forty-First, Forty-Second, Forty-Third, Forty-Fourth —

(*Before SNOG can finish, PAULA, dressed even more extravagantly than on her initial appearance sweeps in.*)

PAULA. Thanks for the intro, Snog, but you forgot Forty-Fifth Street. I'll forgive you this time. (*casual wave of the hand to the monarchs*) Hi, kids. (*PAULA, as MRS. SHRUB did before her, moves into the crowd, shaking hands, introducing herself, making with the small talk.*)

SNOG. (*BANG! BANG! BANG!*) Ladies and gentlemen, His Royal Highness, heir to the throne of Vestigia . . . your future ruler and king . . . Prince Vladimir!

(*A communal squeal goes up from the FEMALES. The CANDIDATES push forward and perform elaborate curtsies as VLAD enters. Whatever his costume, it should include a handsome white jacket or white military tunic — festooned with ribbons and medals.*)

CANDIDATES. Your Royal Highness.
VLAD. Ladies. (*GYPOLA pushes in.*)
GYPOLA. Pick.
VLAD. You forget yourself, Gypola.
GYPOLA. (*to audience*) All I need is one good shot.
KING. (*stands*) Everyone on the terrace for sushi. (*Like a herd of stampeding buffalo, ENSEMBLE dashes offstage, L. All, that is, except for IVY, OLEANDER and MRS. SHRUB, VLAD.*)
MRS. SHRUB. Stay a moment, Your Majesty.
IVY. The sushi will keep.
OLEANDER. I like pizza better than sushi.
IVY. Promise me the next waltz.
OLEANDER. No, I want it. (*VLAD forces himself to be polite. It's a struggle.*)

VLAD. I mustn't neglect my other guests.

MRS. SHRUB. I suppose Gypola has told you I'm wealthy, witty and wise. Emphasis on the *wealthy.* Hee, hee, hee.

VLAD. I believe she mentioned something about it.

IVY. I want a husband. (*MRS. SHRUB smacks IVY with her fan.*)

OLEANDER. Any husband. (*She gets a smack with the fan.*)

MRS. SHRUB. Ha, ha, ha. Aren't my daughters amusing? Actually, you know, Prince — I'm eligible, too.

IVY & OLEANDER. Mama!

MRS. SHRUB. (*fusses with her hair, flirts*) Have you ever considered a more mature type? (*VLAD can tolerate no more.*)

VLAD. You know the rumor about the Charming Curse.

OTHERS. (*making light of the subject*) Ha, ha, ha.

VLAD. It's true.

OTHERS. True?

VLAD. (*declares*) I am a werewolf. (*courteously*) If you'll excuse me. The sushi is waiting. (*He exits. OTHERS stare after him, numb.*)

IVY. Maybe he *was* the wolfman we saw last night.

MRS. SHRUB. I thought the rumor about the prince was only malicious gossip.

OLEANDER. (*to IVY*) We can't marry a wolfman. (*pause*) Can we? (*They look from one to another. Marry a wolfman? It's a thought. MUSIC INTROS, they sing:*)

THE BEAST IN ME

TRIO.
MAYBE A FATE
WITH A WOLF FOR A MATE
IS A BLESSING!
    OLEANDER/IVY.
GIRLS SUCH AS US
CAN'T AFFORD TO BE FUSS-
Y AND COY!
    MRS. SHRUB.
MANY A YEAR HAS SWUM BY!
    OLEANDER.
HE COULD BE OUR LAST STRAW!
    IVY.
PRINCES ARE HARD TO COME BY!

TRIO.
SO WHY OBJECT TO STANDING HAND-IN-PAW?
    OLEANDER.
SHEER COMMON SENSE
FINDS OUR PROSPECTS IMMENSE-
LY DEPRESSING!
    IVY.
FAT IS THE CHANCE
WE'RE A CINCH FOR ROMANCE
WITH A BOY!
    MRS. SHRUB. (*Though far from maidenly, she can dream.*)
MAIDENLY RESERVATION'S CRAMPING OUR *JOIE
    D'ESPRIT!*
(PR. "ZHWA DAY-SPREE" — "BRIGHT SPIRITS")
    TRIO.
A WOLFMAN AT LEAST
OUGHT TO BRING OUT THE BEAST
IN ME!

(*TRIO does little dance for four bars, as MUSIC modulates into
    even brighter melodics, then they continue cheerily:*)

    MRS. SHRUB.
WHY SHOULD WE CARE
IF HIS FACE IS A HAIR
Y DISTORTION?
    OLEANDER/IVY.
LANDING A MALE
WITH A LONG FURRY TAIL
IS OKAY!
    MRS. SHRUB.
MANY A MAN'S A DRINKER!
    OLEANDER.
MANY A HEART THEY BREAK!
    IVY.
MANY A MAN'S A STINKER!
    TRIO.
SO ONE MERE WOLF IS NOT SO HARD TO TAKE!
OH,
NO NEED TO POUT
IF YOU DON'T BLOW IT OUT
OF PROPORTION!
LOOK ON THE BRIGHT

SIDE: HE'S OUT EV'RY NIGHT
UNTIL DAY!
POSSIBLY WE WOULD FIND IT RATHER
ADVENTUROUS!
OLEANDER.
WHILE HE'S ON THE MOOR,
YOU'D BE SAFE AND SECURE!
OLEANDER/MRS. SHRUB.
AND ONCE SUN IS UP,
HE'S AS CUTE AS A PUP!
TRIO.
IF HE'S WELL POLICED,
HE COULD BRING OUT THE BEAST
IN US!
(*MUSIC plays an* obligato, *and—their "paws" (limp-wristed hands) dangling under their chins like a begging canine—they end the song with happy barks of:) Arf-arf!*

(*ENSEMBLE surges back into scene and, more-or-less, takes up previous positions.*)

GIRL #1. Good sushi.
GIRL #2. What there was of it.
GIRL #3. They ran out of pickles.
MRS. SHRUB. (*to VLAD*) There you are again, Prince.
VLAD. (*resigned*) Here I am again.
MRS. SHRUB. (*confidential tone*) Don't worry about a thing. I've talked it over with my daughters and everything's all right. They have no objections. (*a terrible attempt at humor*) But remember—I get the pick of the litter. Hee, hee, hee. (*VLAD frowns, frees himself as SNOG bangs the staff: BANG! BANG! BANG!*)
SNOG. An uninvited guest.
AD LIBS.
Uninvited guest?
Who can it be?
No one's supposed to arrive after the prince.
Can you see?

(*Again, SNOG bangs the staff: BANG! BANG! BANG! (NOTE: CINDERELLA will enter U.R. so it's important that the audience has an unobstructed view. Her entrance to the royal ball* is the highlight of the spoof.) *Pause for effect, and then: CIN-DERELLA appears. She is lovely, gowned beautifully, wears a sparkling pair of dancing slippers. She is the most radiant creature in the palace. PAULA has done her work well. This is a complete metamorphosis — from kitchen slavey to mysterious beauty. From the sidelines, PAULA beams. So no one will suspect who she is, CINDERELLA wears a mask. She floats in front of the dais and curtsies to the KING and QUEEN.)*

KING. What a delightful creature.

QUEEN. I wonder who she is?

KING. What are you waiting for, Vlad? Select a partner and dance.

PAULA. Good idea, King. Everybody dance. Let's get with it.

(Each of the CANDIDATES smiles, hoping the prince will select her. However, he's been attracted by the late arrival. There's something about her . . . ? He steps to CINDERELLA and offers his hand. She looks up and is amazed to see the chef she loves is in reality — PRINCE CHARMING.)

CINDERELLA. *(surprised; to audience)* It's him! The chef who helped me with the luggage. It's magic. *(She accepts VLAD's hand. CANDIDATES, disappointed, moan. The dancing begins again.)*

LOVELY PEOPLE, LOVELY . . . SWINE?

ALL BUT CINDERELLA.
(horribly slow and dreary)
LOVELY PEOPLE IN A LOVELY WALTZ,
THROBBING PULSES DOING SOMERSAULTS
AS WITH THE MUSIC WE'RE SLOWLY SWEPT AWAY,
CAPTURING ENRAPTURING DELIGHTS WHERE WE
    MAY!
CINDERELLA.
(cannot take another moment of it; pulls free of VLAD's arms, and MUSIC pauses as she shouts) Hooooold it! *(DANCERS stop, stare at her in amazement as she chides VLAD.)* You may be havin' a ball, Prince, but *I'm* not! My *foot's* going to sleep, and if

the music stays *this* dreary, I may *follow it*! Why, when I'm sloppin' the *hogs* at home, *they* dance better than *this*!

VLAD. (*entranced by her, but bewildered*) You're joking! . . . Aren't you?

CINDERELLA. I can *prove* it! (*to DANCERS:*) I want *everybody* to sing "shnork"!

DANCERS. (*incredulous*) "Shnork?!"

CINDERELLA. (*arms akimbo, shrugs calmly*) I was *only* quotin' the *pigs!*

VLAD. (*springing to the defense of this ravishing creature*) By royal decree — *everybody* shnork! (*IGOR steps forward with pitch pipe and blows so singers will know where to start.*)

DANCERS.
(*obediently begin to sing an underbeat-tempo repetition of:*)
SHNORK! SHNORK! SHNORK! SHNORK-SHNORK! (*etc.*)
CINDERELLA.
(*starts grotesque hoedown-step as she over-sings:*)
STEP AROUND THAT MOUND OF MUD! OSCILLATE
   YOUR SPINE!
PUT YOUR HOOF DOWN WITH A THUD! OINK-OINK!
YOU'RE DOIN' *THE SWINE!*
VLAD.
(*caught up in her high spirits*)
TIPPY-TOE UP TO THE SWILL! LET YOUR TAILS
   ENTWINE!
WHO THE HECK NEEDS CHLOROPHYLL! OINK-OINK!
YOU'RE DOIN' *THE SWINE!* (*Now DANCERS stop
   undersinging as ACCOMPANIMENT starts, and they go
   as crazily into the spirit as VLAD did.*)
DANCERS.
LEAN YOUR ELBOWS ON THE TROUGH WITH A SIGH!
CINDERELLA/VLAD.
HAVE A SWALLOW!
WHY BE HOLLOW?
DANCERS.
SCRATCH YOUR BACK AGAINST THE SIDE OF THE
   STY!
CINDERELLA/VLAD.
WHILE YOU WALLOW!
ALL.
FACE YOUR NEIGHBOR SNOUT-TO-SNOUT

JUST FOR AULD LANG SYNE!
CHASE EACH OTHER ROUND ABOUT!
OINK-OINK! YOU'RE DOIN' *THE SWINE!*
(*Now ALL dance with wild porcine enthusiasm; when
dance-interval is done, we return to the singing with:*)
CINDERELLA/VLAD.
SO LEAVE THE PIGPEN SEEKING SOFTER DEBRIS!
DANCERS.
TRY TO SNUFFLE
WHILE YOU SHUFFLE!
CINDERELLA/VLAD.
IF YOU SHOULD BUMP UP AGAINST AN OAK
TREE . . .
DANCERS.
. . . DIG THAT TRUFFLE!
ALL.
GARBAGE HEAPS ARE NUMBER ONE
WHEN IT'S TIME TO DINE!
IT'S A PIG'S LIFE, BUT IT'S FUN!
SPLISH-SPLOSH! THE PUDDLES ARE FINE!
SQUISH-SQUASH! THE MUD IS DIVINE!
WATERPROOF YOUR HOOF,
YOU'RE DOIN' *THE SWINE!*
THE SWINE! THE SWINE!
(*Then ALL embrace partners and finish dreamily:*)
AND YOU'RE MINE . . . !

VLAD. Sloppin' the hogs at home? Ha ha. You have a gift for humor. I like that. You have warmed my lonely heart. I feel I know you well.

KING. Marry her, Vlad.

QUEEN. Marry her at once.

GYPOLA. (*to audience*) Is she one of my clients?

CINDERELLA. The dance was lovely, Prince Vladimir, I shall never forget it.

VLAD. What good fortune. Not only are you mysterious and lovely and down to earth — you are rich.

CINDERELLA. Alas, you must forget me. I don't have a cent. (*ALL gasp.*)

IGOR. She slops hogs all day and she doesn't have a cent (scent)? (*to audience*) Don't blame me. I don't write these lines.

CINDERELLA. I must leave. Farewell, my Prince.

VLAD. Farewell? You're not serious.

CINDERELLA. Farewell, farewell! (*CINDERELLA runs off, U.R.*)

VLAD. No, come back! (*Pause, then—one of CINDER-ELLA's dancing shoes flies back onto the stage and hits with a thud. To OTHERS—*) Who *was* that masked woman? (*He retrieves the shoe. Pause, then—*) I have made my selection. (*ALL lean forward.*)

ALL. Yes?

VLAD. I will marry the girl whose foot fits this shoe.

GYPOLA. (*all business*) All right, girls, you heard him. Line up.

VLAD. How's that?

GYPOLA. We all heard you. You said you were going to marry the girl whose foot fits that shoe.

VLAD. What if I did?

GYPOLA. A prince can't go back on his word.

QUEEN. She's right, Vlad.

KING. It's the law of Vestigia.

SNIG. It's never been done.

SNOG. It would set a bad precedent.

VLAD. But I meant the girl in the mask!

GYPOLA. Tough.

VLAD. (*tragically*) What a strange twist of fate. (*GYPOLA is busy getting the CANDIDATES into a line.*)

GYPOLA. Line up, line up. You here . . . you here . . . you're next. Everyone's got a chance. No shoving, no pushing.

VLAD. (*to KING and QUEEN*) Must I? (*They nod that he must. A reluctant VLAD gets down on one knee, holding CINDERELLA's dancing slipper. Each CANDIDATE slips off her shoe and attempts to squeeze into the slipper. The slipper is too tiny for any of them. As each CANDIDATE struggles, OTHERS lean forward. When VLAD shakes his head, GYPOLA roars out "NEXT!" . . . shoe-fitting business, "NEXT!" . . . shoe-fitting business, "NEXT!", etc. Last in line are IVY and OLEANDER.*)

IVY. It'll fit, it'll fit.

MRS. SHRUB. Push, dear. Shove. Stuff. Squeeze.

IVY. I'm shoving, I'm stuffing, I'm squeezing. (*attempts to force a fit*) Ow, oh, ah.

OLEANDER. (*pushes her sister aside*) Let me try. (*OLEANDER makes an attempt and ONLOOKERS encourage her with —*)

ONLOOKERS. *Push! Shove! Stuff! Squeeze! (OLEANDER gives it her best, groaning with the effort. It's no go. Still, she won't give up.)*

OLEANDER. It's going to fit! It's going to fit! Almost on! (*The slipper dangles from her toes.*) There! You see. It fits! (*Laughter from ONLOOKERS.*)

VLAD. It does not fit, Miss Sumac.

OLEANDER. (*bawls*) Oleander, not Sumac. Auuuuuuugh . . . (*OLEANDER steps to her mother for comfort.*)

MRS. SHRUB. There, there. Don't cry. It's all palace politics.

VLAD. (*stands*) I *must* find the girl whose dainty foot fits this dainty slipper. (*CINDERELLA, now wearing her rags, appears* D.L. *with a broom, no shoes.*)

PAULA. Try the shoe on her.

OTHERS. On who? (*She points. ALL look to CINDERELLA.*)

IVY. That's Cinderella. Our servant.

OLEANDER. A serving girl for a prince?

IVY, OLEANDER, MRS. SHRUB. Ha, ha, ha.

VLAD. The girl who thinks I work here as a chef. (*to audience*) This shoe . . . wouldn't it be wonderful if it fit? Alas, that is too much to hope for.

PAULA. Ah, go on, Prince. Give it a try. What have you got to lose?

VLAD. It shall be done.

QUEEN. Move along, child.

KING. Try on the dancing slipper. (*Dutiful, CINDERELLA puts down the broom, and crosses to the prince. He gets down on one knee and slowly . . . building for impact . . . he fits the slipper.*)

SNOG. It fits!

ONLOOKERS. *It fits! (All but CANDIDATES and MOTHERS break into applause and cheers, etc. NOTE: Funny bit if the shoe has a heel. Thus, when CINDERELLA "walks," she's lopsided.*)

VLAD. (*stands*) You were the masked beauty.

CINDERELLA. (*with admiration*) I owe everything to Paula Pond.

PAULA. Anytime.

IVY. Who'd have thought our stepsister would be a princess.

OLEANDER. It's not fair.

VLAD. You ought to be ashamed of yourselves. I could have

you both thrown in the dungeon or sent to the guillotine for treating your sister so harshly. (*romantic*) Do you truly love me, Cinderella?

CINDERELLA. As prince . . . as man . . . as werewolf.

ONLOOKERS. *Werewolf!?*

VLAD. Then you know?

CINDERELLA. Uh-huh. That ring on your finger. (*VLAD displays the ring.*) You were wearing it when we first met. (*to OTHERS*) When the wolfman ran down the garden passageway, he was wearing that same ring.

VLAD. What a clever girl.

CINDERELLA. (*bats her eyelashes*) I know.

PAULA. You mean all this wolfman stuff I've been hearing is for real?

SNOG. It is.

PAULA. (*to CINDERELLA and VLAD*) In that case, kids, I'd advise you to live in London. It's always raining and foggy there. There's never any moon.

CINDERELLA. (*smiling with cheery stupidity*) *And,* as everybody knows, *the sun never sets on the British Empire!*

SNIG. But we're back where we started from, Your Majesties. This girl is penniless. Not a sou.

SNOG. Not a kopeck.

GYPOLA. She doesn't have two peasants to rub together.

MAN'S VOICE. (*From offstage,* U.L.) *Cinderella has all the money in the kingdom! (All look* U.L.)

ONLOOKERS. Who? What?

(*MAN enters with a parachute in his arms. He wears some kind of ragged aviator's uniform, goggles on his forehead. He marches* DS.)

MRS. SHRUB. *Walter!*

CINDERELLA. *Father!* (*She embraces him.*) I thought you were gone forever.

MAN. The air currents blew me off course. I landed in Cincinnati and had to walk back. I'm pooped.

MRS. SHRUB. (*also embraces him*) Walter, I was so distressed about you that I was inconsiderate to Cinderella. (*ALL look into audience and nod knowingly at this ridiculous comment. NOTE: From this point on, one absurdity piles on top of the next.*)

PAULA. This will make a great film and I'll be the star.

IGOR. I've always wanted to go to Hollywood.

PAULA. You're in luck. Just so happens I'm in the need of a new agent. You're the right type.

IGOR. What type is that?

PAULA. Horrible.   ·

IGOR. Oh, thank you!

IVY & OLEANDER. We want to be married.

CINDERELLA. Easily arranged. Snig and Snog.

SNIG & SNOG. Forget it. No way.

CINDERELLA. Father, you'll give Ivy and Oleander a wedding dowry, won't you?

MAN. I'll settle fortunes on the men who marry them.

SNIG & SNOG. We accept.

CANDIDATES. What about us?

GYPOLA. Don't worry, girls. I'll go to Transylvania and dig something up.

IGOR. I wish I could remember what I forgot.

GYPOLA. (*saving her neck*) If you forgot it's not worth remembering.

KING. (*stands*) Vestigia is saved!

OTHERS. *Hooray!*

(*NOTE: For the finale everyone but GYPOLA is "paired off"—
    CINDERELLA and VLAD, IVY and SNOG, OLEANDER
    and SNIG, KING and QUEEN, PAULA and IGOR, MITZI
    and RODOLPHO, MAN and MRS. SHRUB, etc. MUSIC
    INTROS, and:*)

IF THE SHOE FITS . . .

ALL.
IF THE SHOE FITS, WEAR IT!
THIS COULD BE YOUR NIGHT!
TRY TO GRIN AND BEAR IT
IF IT'S SLIGHTLY TIGHT!
YOU'LL FIND THE STRAIN
(THOUGH IT CAN MAKE YOU WINCE)
WELL WORTH THE PAIN
WHEN YOU'RE LANDING A PRINCE!
    GYPOLA.
NOW THOSE NASTY SISTERS'
PLANS HAVE GONE ASKEW!

KING AND QUEEN.
ALL THEY GOT WERE BLISTERS
FROM THAT TINY SHOE!
    MRS. SHRUB/FATHER.
PUSHING AND SHOVING
WITH FEET MUCH TOO BIG
WON THEM NO LOVING
EXCEPT SNOG AND SNIG!
    CHORUS.
CINDERELLA WAS SKITTISH
TO WIN HER FELLA TONIGHT!
    CINDERELLA/VLAD.
SO WE'RE GONNA BE BRITISH,
WITH NO FEAR FROM THE MOONLIGHT!
    SNIG/OLEANDER.
OUR FATE IS GOOD, BUT IT COULD HAVE BEEN
    GROOVY!
    SNOG/IVY.
AT LEAST WE STILL ARE ALIVE TO RESPOND!
    PAULA/IGOR.
WHEN HOLLYWOOD MAKES THIS INTO A MOVIE,
LET HOPE THE FILM'S STAR WILL BE PAULA POND!
    SNIG.
FAIRYTALE PLOT-LINES HAVE NEVER BEEN
    STRANGER!
    SNIG/OLEANDER.
A SCARY DEMISE NEARLY OVERTOOK HER!
    SNIG/OLEANDER/IVY.
HAIRY MALE HABITS ARE NO LONGER DANGEROUS:
    SNIG/OLEANDER/IVY/SNOG.
SHE HAD THE CLOSE SHAVE, BUT HE LOST THE FUR!
    MITZI/RODOLPHO.
GUYS AND GALS HAVE SQUARED OFF!
FUTURE'S LOOKING FAIR!
EV'RYBODY'S PAIRED OFF!
LOVE IS IN THE AIR!
    PAULA. (*to IGOR*)
THOUGH YOU LOOK SAPPY,
I LOVE YOU A BUNCH!
    IGOR. (*to PAULA*)
VE VILL BE HAPPY,
DEAR, I'FE GOT A HUNCH!

ALL MEN.
WHY ARE WE STANDING HERE TRYING TO SING
 DUMB
LYRICS WHEN WE COULD BE KISSING OUR BRIDES?
 ALL WOMEN.
DUTY'S DEMANDING WE FAVOR THE KINGDOM
OVER OUR BOYFRIENDS WHO PANT BY OUR SIDES!
 QUEEN/KING.
FINANCES ARE NEW-BORN!
SON, WE'RE FILLED WITH PRIDE!
 OLEANDER/IVY.
IF WE'D HAD A SHOE-HORN,
WE'D HAVE BEEN HIS BRIDE!
 MRS. SHRUB/FATHER.
LIFE HAS NEW ZIP!
WARMER ARMS NOW BEWITCH!
 CINDERELLA(VLAD).
DEAR (YOUR) DADDY'S RIP-
CORD HAS RENDERED US RICH!
 ALL.
LET'S HALT THE ENTERTAINING,
AND IN THE TIME REMAINING
TURN, AND WITH PULSES RACING,
START SERIOUS EMBRACING!
(*COUPLES embrace now, but still face out front.*)
LET'S NOT RUN OUT OF PATIENCE!
LET'S LET THOSE OSCULATIONS
BLEND!
SINCE THE STUPID SHOE FITS, MAY WE RECOMMEND:
BRING THIS STORY TO ITS HAPPY END!

(*And ALL COUPLES kiss* [a quick *lip-peck, not a big smooch,
    since there is allotted only a single music-beat for it*] *on final
    chord of song.*)

End of Musical Spoof

PRODUCTION NOTES

PROPERTIES:

ON STAGE THROUGHOUT: Two throne-like chairs on a dais, 2 benches, casement window.

ACT ONE, brought on: Cap with card reading "GUIDE" stuck on (TOUR GUIDE), cameras and guide books (TOURISTS), stick with bells attached (Jester's stick), watch, water tap on string, bottle of "PRIDE" (IGOR), pearls (QUEEN), large ring (VLAD), whistle, silver bullet, rifle (GYPOLA), pompons (CHORUS), luggage, wicker hamper or chest (CINDERELLA), "moon" on a pole (CAST MEMBER).

ACT TWO, Scene 1, brought on: Ball gown for sewing, two water buckets (CINDERELLA), luggage containing fancy dress or ball gown, gloves, jewels, wig, hand mirror (MITZI & RODOLPHO), rifle (GYPOLA).

ACT TWO, Scene 2, brought on: Majordomo staff (SNOG), mask, broom (CINDERELLA), whistle (IGOR), parachute, goggles (MAN).

COSTUMES

Most of the special needs are mentioned into text. Since the time period is contemporary, modern clothing will work. KING and QUEEN can wear a sash over their overfits to indicate their station in Act One. CASTLE STAFF can wear white jackets (MALES) or aprons and caps (MAIDS). Naturally, the royal ball costumes should be as pretty to the eye as you can manage. The big costume consideration is Cinderella's ball gown. *It must be a knockout.*

FLEXIBLE CASTING

Various characters can easily "double" (even triple). For example the FEMALE TOURISTS can become GUESTS at the ball — even MARRIAGE CANDIDATES. GUIDE can play RODOLPHO. Cinderella's father can play the WOLFMAN. The CASTLE STAFF, if necessary, can be only one steward and one maid. Actress who plays PAULA can, in Act One, play a MOTHER, as can MITZI, etc. FARMER can also play GUIDE or CASTLE STAFF, or FARMER can be played as a female role. The point being, do whatever is required to fit your needs. It doesn't hurt one bit, in fact it's good for a laugh, if audience sees a character playing several roles.

CINDERELLA MEETS THE WOLFMAN IS NOT A SUBTLE SHOW!

SOUND: Thunder.

SPECIAL LIGHTING EFFECTS: Blackout for Wolfman "transformation scene," romantic lighting for royal ball.

MISCELLANEOUS

DRESSING UP THE SET

Depending on your resources, anything can be added to give additional "atmosphere": flags, large potted plants, canopy over the thrones, chandelier, etc.

THE MOON COMES UP

(For the "prince-into-wolfman" sequence): The moon is not absolutely necessary — a shaft of concentrated brightness from the wings to "suggest" moonlight will suffice. However, an actual moon that the audience can see proves most effective. It also enables Vlad to "react" on seeing it. If the moon can be dropped from the overhead flies, good. If not, have some cast member step behind the casement window when the marriage candidates pull in the prince prior to "My Night To Howl." The cast member will carry the "moon" on a pole. At the indicated moment the "moon will rise." The cornier the effect the better.

PRINCE INTO WOLFMAN

This business is carefully orchestrated in the number "My Night To Howl." Of course, it requires ANOTHER ACTOR already made up as the wolfman to represent Vlad the beastie. He, too, wears a chefs uniform. No hat. As soon as the BLACKOUT hits, Vlad ducks from sight (either behind the throne, or a fast dash into the wings) — and the double takes his place. If you experience any difficulty with this blocking, instead of Vlad standing on the thrones have actor move STAGE RIGHT so when the BLACKOUT hits he simply EXITS to be replaced by the wolf.

However, the best bet is to follow the stage directions as written and have the actor on the thrones.

REMEMBER — the "wilder" the wolfman looks, the bigger the laugh at Act One curtain. Gnashing teeth, a bush of scattered hair, furry face, black wet nose, pointed ears, long-clawed paws, a tail.

GUIDELINES/SUGGESTIONS FOR THE STAGING OF CERTAIN SONGS

"BANKRUPTCY!": For optimum comic effect, mix your baritones, contraltos, tenors and sopranos so no one is standing next to another of his/her same vocal level. Then, give each group its own set of "calisthenics" to accompany their individual lyrics. It need not be complicated; baritones, for instance, could do "Bank-rupt-cy" with a mournful left-right-left head-tilt, and then on "the kingdom's in" could do a thrust-out-in-front hand-wringing, then back to head-tilts for "bank-rupt-cy" again, and so forth. Contraltos could then fling hands sadly overhead for "We got no cash!" and then stretch hands out palms-up-and-empty for "We got no dough!" and so forth. Similar *simple*-but-visual bits of business-per-lyric can then be contrived for the tenors and sopranos (nothing vigorous enough to move them out of their lineup). Each vocal group must be *motionless,* however, when *not* singing. By the time all four voices are inter-mixing, the overall visual effect is hilarious, resembling an "aerobics class gone berserk". At *final* line "If they blend/there'll be/a sudden end/to bankruptcy!", as each group sings its own segment, they should do a step-forward-and-down-on-one-knee movement with hands outstretched toward audience; when all four are down, on the final shout of "Whee!" all four groups should *leap up* into the air, and land with a *ta-dah* stance, to reap maximum applause on the finish.

"HAVĒ I GOT A GIRL FOR YOU!": Now, pompons are fun to watch in motion, but they are also quite *distracting,* so in this song when CHORUS enters, be sure their pompons are out of view behind their backs; the *first* time we'll see those pompons is when the CHORUS sings "Oh, golly!" Thenceforth, pompons will be shaken only when *CHORUS* is singing, *not* during any of GYPOLA's lead-in lines, and *especially* not during "interview" segments of song, when VLAD is going one-on-one with each candidate; during these interview segments, only VLAD and current candidate should move at all; GYPOLA and CHORUS should stand as if frozen into stone, only coming "out of paralysis" as they react to each candidate's final (and always distressing) punchline. In this way, the audience will always be focused on the important part of the song, and be looking in the right area at the right time. During *coda* of song, however, pompons can go crazy.

"IT WAS A WOLF!": Unlike the "BANKRUPTCY!" number cited above, *this* song derives its maximum effect if the disparate groups *are* with their own faction, PEASANTS and PALACE singers facing one another as if they were rival debating teams, one group angled from upstage center to downstage left, the other from upstage center to downstage right. This way, the audience can easily follow this "musical tennis match" as the accusations and counter-accusations fly back and forth, and any overlap-lyrics won't be "muddied" by being intermingled with contrasting lyrics by the opposing faction; the audience must *always* know which group sings what.

"IF THE SHOE FITS — ": Since the show's finale is a madcap conga/samba, the entire company should be *dancing* as soon as the musical intro ends and the lyrics begin, partnered by couples wherever possible (GYPOLA is the only principal without a partner). *However,* any time an individual or a couple have *solo*-lyrics (that is, when ALL are not singing a particular line) that person or those persons should step *down front* for that segment of the lyric, so that the audience does not have to "scan" the company to determine who is singing a particular line; this is especially important in the "plot-wrapup" segments (such as PAULA/IGOR's exchange ending with his "I've got a *hunch!*" — it's only funny if the audience knows *who* is singing the line). Since this finale wraps up the plot, the romances, and all the "loose ends" of the story-line, don't deprive the audience of the chance to *hear* the lyrics; hence that down-front singer-position. Of course, once each person/couple *finishes* their lyric, they quickly rejoin the company so that *next* person/couple can come down-front, etc., for the ideal comic/communicative effect.

CURTAIN-CALL MUSIC: The OVERTURE should serve as ideal backup as chorus members, then principals, come onstage and take group-or-individual bows; with *precise* timing, all your principals will have *finished* bowing just before the music comes to the "IF THE SHOE FITS" coda, so that the entire company can start *dancing* as the curtain closes, leaving the audience cheering and applauding like crazy for a *very* long time. (If it's for an *extremely* long time, raise [or open] the curtain and take another company-bow. You've earned it.)

OTHER SONG-NUMBERS: The remainder of the score's

songs' staging is described in detail in both the text of the script *and* in the piano/conductor score itself (such as that interruption in mid-waltz by CINDERELLA during "LOVELY PEOPLE, LOVELY . . . SWINE?"), so there's no need to detail them more thoroughly here. It's a fun-show for both cast *and* audience. Enjoy!

OTHER TITLES AVAILABLE FROM SAMUEL FRENCH

LITTLE GREEN MEN

Book, Music and Lyrics by Scott Martin

Musical Comedy / 4m, 5f, plus 2m child, 2f child

Several young campers and their adult counselors are stranded at a mountaintop wilderness retreat on the night of October 30th, 1938. When someone switches on the radio to Orson Welles' *War Of The Worlds* live broadcast, the night that panics America also becomes the night that panics Camp gitchiegoomie. Are little green men from Mars actually surrounding the mess hall, ready to make a mess of everyone inside? Can the feuding boys and girls work together to save themselves from the mysterious alien invasion? And why is that strange hairy, bug-eyed monster lurking in the bushes?

This hilarious, family-friendly musical recreates the innocent fun and slapstick humor of the wise-cracking, high-spirited film comedies of the late 1930s, complete with spooky campfires, ghostly shadows, hair-raising Halloween surprises and the scariest radio play of all time that nearly fooled the entire nation. The lively, toe-tapping original songs are fondly reminiscent of the popular scores from the golden age of the Warner Brothers and MGM film musicals with plenty of high-kicking, energetic and imaginative choreography in the unforgettable styles of Busby Berkeley, Fred Astaire and Gene Kelly.

This happiest-of-Halloween musical comedies is guaranteed fun for the entire family, from the youngest monster movie fan to the oldest senior who actually experienced that memorable night breathlessly cowered in front of the radio when the world was "invaded" by Little Green Men.

"A boisterous musical. The catchy, innovative music embellished with slapstick humor makes for funny stuff. The whole family should see this charming play."
–*The Los Angeles Easy Reader*